IN DEFENSE OF GUN CONTROL

IN DEFENSE OF GUN CONTROL

Hugh LaFollette

OXFORD
UNIVERSITY PRESS

OXFORD
UNIVERSITY PRESS

Oxford University Press is a department of the University of Oxford. It furthers
the University's objective of excellence in research, scholarship, and education
by publishing worldwide. Oxford is a registered trade mark of Oxford University
Press in the UK and certain other countries.

Published in the United States of America by Oxford University Press
198 Madison Avenue, New York, NY 10016, United States of America.

CIP data is on file at the Library of Congress
ISBN 978-0-19-087337-0 (pbk.)
ISBN 978-0-19-087336-3 (hbk.)

1 3 5 7 9 8 6 4 2

Paperback printed by Webcom, Inc., Canada
Hardback printed by Bridgeport National Bindery, Inc., United States of America

CONTENTS

PREFACE

I grew up in a gun culture. My father was an avid hunter and an amateur gun collector. He had multiple handguns, rifles, and shotguns. To me that seemed normal. As a teenager, I assumed I would continue that tradition. Hence, when my dad gave me a shotgun for my thirteenth birthday I was ecstatic. My father's gift meant that he saw me as a man; I could now join him when he went hunting. It is difficult to overstate the satisfaction and self-esteem his gift bestowed.

When I became an adult and moved out on my own, I was no longer enamored of guns; but, then, neither was I an ardent critic of private gun ownership. Although I had thought, both personally and professionally, about a wide range of moral and political issues, gun control was not among them. That changed in the mid-1990s when I spent the academic year at the University of Stirling in Scotland. While exploring housing options for my sabbatical, a disgruntled forty-three-year-old resident of Stirling drove to the elementary school in the neighboring village of Dunblane where he shot and killed sixteen children and one teacher; he wounded many others. When we moved to Stirling three months later, the community was reeling from the massacre. There were few Dunblane residents who had not been personally affected by this slaughter of the innocents. During our year, we learned details about several families whose children were killed. We sensed the citizens' confusion, anger, and profound grief when we frequented one of their local pubs. I met and became friendly with the solicitor (attorney) who represented the parents of the children killed in the massacre. Suddenly the issue of gun control was real in a way that it had never been before. My disease at having no settled view of the topic nagged at me for several years before I decided that agnosticism on this topic was neither intellectually tenable nor morally responsible. I was impelled to examine the arguments and the evidence to reach a fair and informed view.

Confronting this issue carefully, thoughtfully, and honestly is not easy in the United States where the public debate about the private ownership of guns is contentious, often nasty, and rarely insightful. I had to make a serious effort to identify the most plausible views for and against gun control. One of the first things I noted was that this way of framing the debate grotesquely oversimplifies it. I explain why and how in chapter 1. I had to read and reread the available literature so that I could understand the armchair, rights-based, and empirical arguments concerning the control of privately owned guns. Only then would I be prepared to assess the evidence and reach an informed—even if tentative—conclusion. Unfortunately, since most philosophers were like me, there was little extant literature. Outside of the public arena—where most arguments are simplistic, and too many are demonstrably unfair, or blatant ad hominems—the bulk of available literature on the topic came from physicians, social scientists, and public health professionals.

Having absorbed that literature, I sought to separate the rhetorical chaff from the substantive argumentative wheat. With any issue that is difficult to do, in part because advocates "on the same side" tend to hold somewhat divergent positions. So I sought to identify not only the variations but also the common beliefs and claims characterizing those who embrace and those who oppose gun control.

The hope for any progress on this topic within our culture requires civil, honest, and fair discussion, not schoolyard name-calling. People who disagree should listen to what opponents say and should be willing to alter their views in the face of compelling evidence. Of course, that is easier said than done. We are all subject to the confirmation bias, the tendency to look for evidence that supports views we already embrace. Overcoming this bias requires diligence and honest self-criticism. We should impartially assess the arguments and evidence. We should recognize and acknowledge the strengths of competing arguments, even if we decide, in the end, that they are not convincing.

This book is my attempt to understand and accurately describe the options, to identify a plausible resolution, and then to vigorously defend that conclusion, to show why I find it superior to the alternatives.

ACKNOWLEDGMENTS

For helping me viscerally appreciate the issues, I thank my father, who was an avid gun enthusiast, and Scottish solicitor Peter Watson, who represented the parents of the children slaughtered at the Dunblane primary school. I thank the two anonymous reviewers for the press for their incisive comments and suggestions. I thank my editor, Peter Ohlin, for his encouragement and thoughtful comments, and for good naturedly enduring my idiosyncratic approach to philosophical writing and publishing. I thank OUP editorial assistant Abigail Johnson for her patience, assistance, and efficiency.

I thank my wife and best friend, Eva LaFollette, for numerous insights, thoughtful questions, and unfailing encouragement from the inception to completion of this project.

I thank Jeff McMahan, who encouraged me to write this book and made painstaking commentary on all early chapters. I thank David DeGrazia for sharing his innovative work on the topic, and for giving me some sage advice as I completed the manuscript. I thank David Hemenway, who graciously checked my descriptions of the empirical evidence to ensure that I did not mis-describe anyone's view.

I am grateful to Daniel Mosley for his helpful comments on several chapters, and George Rainbolt for extensive comments on chapter 3.

Finally, I thank a cadre of St. Petersburg citizens who listened and offered valuable feedback on my first attempts to develop the arguments contained herein. I especially thank Allan Roit, Diana Craig, George Sherman, John Funke, Renne Proulx, Rich Rome, Sue Nigro, and Tina Spangler.

IN DEFENSE OF GUN CONTROL

Chapter 1

Understanding the Issues

On March 13, 1996, Thomas Hamilton took four handguns into a primary (elementary) school in Dunblane, Scotland, where he killed sixteen children and one adult, wounded fifteen others, and then killed himself. The UK public responded by overwhelmingly supporting two laws that made the private ownership of handguns within one's home or on one's person effectively illegal throughout Britain. The public wanted to ensure that such a senseless massacre would never happen again.

On December 14, 2012, after killing his mother, Adam Lanza walked into the Sandy Hook Elementary School in Connecticut and killed twenty children and six adults—and wounded two others—before committing suicide. Although six US states did strengthen their gun control laws after this tragedy, the national government passed no new guns laws. That was never a serious possibility.

Nonetheless, in both countries, these events prompted intensified conversations about and advocacy for more serious gun control measures not seen in years. The common factor in both cases was that very young children died; many others were wounded; all present were traumatized. Citizens who had been relatively unmoved by spree killings at Virginia Tech, the Tucson Mall, or the Aurora movie theater, were stirred by the slaughter of innocent children.

In the United States, although the Newtown school shooting moved most citizens, many disagreed about the appropriate response. Some citizens saw the massacre as incontrovertible evidence of the need for stricter gun control. "Surely," they said, "we cannot stand by and do nothing." In contrast, the National Rifle Association (NRA), and many of its supporters in Congress, saw this event not as a reason to expand gun control, but as irrefutable reason for arming even more citizens. They asserted that if teachers and custodial staff had been armed, then these law-abiding citizens could have stopped these tragic killings before they happened—or at least before too many children were killed (LaPierre, W. 2013).

These diametrically opposed reactions reflect many Americans' assumption that there are only two options: one must either oppose or support gun control.

THE COMPLEXITY OF OUR OPTIONS

Put differently, most Americans appear to think that if one supports gun control, then the control must be extensive, and if one supports a right to bear arms, then the right must be (almost) unqualified. Both assertions grotesquely misrepresent our choices. Unfortunately, even many people who recognize that this dichotomy oversimplifies the options nonetheless assume that we have only a few alternatives. After all, most public discussion of guns and gun control focuses on a handful of specific proposals.

In fact, we have a plethora of options, more than I can possibly consider in detail. The complexity emerges because available choices and policies do not lie along a single continuum but along five intersecting and overlapping ones. The first three describe public policy issues; the latter two describe individuals' choices in light of those policies. Explaining the nature of each scale reveals the complexity of the debate about gun control. It gives shape to the options we should explore when rationally discussing the issue.

The first policy continuum concerns which classes/groups of individuals we should permit to own firearms. This continuum moves from the view that we should permit all groups of people to own firearms, through the view that we should permit some groups to own firearms, to the position that we should not permit any group of people to own guns. Despite the tendency to think in terms of extremes, few people think we should permit everyone to, or bar everyone from, owning guns. Few think we should permit two-year-olds, former felons (especially former violent felons), or those who are demonstrably mentally ill from owning guns. Others also want to exclude noncitizens and those with no training in gun safety (Wheeler, S. C., III 2001).

The second policy continuum concerns which types of firearms (handguns, shotguns, assault weapons, mortars, tanks, etc.) we should permit private citizens to own. This scale moves from the view that we should allow private individuals who are permitted to own guns to own any type of gun, through the position that we should allow them to privately own only *some* subclass(es) of guns, to the view that we should not permit anyone to privately own any type of firearm. Unless specified otherwise, I use "ownership" as short for "private ownership," and I use "firearms" and "guns" interchangeably.

The third and most complex policy continuum concerns restrictions on firearms that some citizens can legitimately own according to the first two continua. This scale includes regulatory measures required to enforce limits set by those continua. Furthermore, it stipulates when, where, and how those who legitimately own them can purchase or otherwise obtain firearms; how, when, to whom they can sell or transfer them; whether (and how) they can carry them in public; whether these gun owners must be trained; and how they should store guns and ammunition.

This continuum moves from the view that we should not have any restrictions on those guns people can legitimately own, through the position that we should have some restrictions on legitimately owned guns, to the view that we should erect absolute restrictions on these guns. We can best understand the third continuum as comprising a series of subcontinua since each restriction can vary in both content and strength. Not surprisingly, virtually everyone holds a position somewhere between the two extremes.

The fourth and fifth continua concern individual action rather than public policy; hence, they play a minimal role in this book. Nonetheless, any thorough account of gun control should consider the individual dimensions of the debate. The fourth concerns the prudential wisdom of owning a gun. This scale ranges from the position that it is *always wise* to privately own a gun, through the view that it is *sometimes wise*, to the extreme that it is *never wise*—owning a gun is always imprudent. The fifth scale is moral. The scale ranges from the position that it is *always morally permissible* to own firearms, through the view that it is *sometimes morally permissible*, to the other extreme that it is *never morally permissible*. This last scale masks another dimension: some people might assert that people are not just morally *permitted* but morally *required* to own guns.

There is one final dimension of the fourth and fifth scales. Whether one thinks that it is prudent or moral for someone to own a firearm depends in part on the type of firearm in question. Thus, one could ask whether it is prudent, permissible, or obligatory to own each type of weapon: howitzers, mortars, grenades, assault weapons, shotguns, rifles, and various types of handguns.

With these diverse continua at hand, we see that the options are captured by the intermingling of the five scales: we must determine who can legally, prudentially, and morally own firearms; which firearms they can own; and how firearms can be acquired or transferred; whether, where, and how they can be carried; and where and how they must be stored. We must choose options along each continuum. The resulting options are sets of five points, one along each continuum.

Although I will do little more than mention the continua concerning prudential and moral choices, they lurk in the background of the policy debates. Some people might contend that there is a serious *claim* to bear arms, that is, they may think that the government generally has no business interfering with private gun ownership, while also thinking that it is decidedly imprudent, and possibly immoral, for most citizens to own guns.

Such a person might believe that although they have a claim to bear arms, acting on that claim would be imprudent since owning guns is dangerous to themselves and their families; they might also decide it is immoral because having many privately owned guns is dangerous to others. Nonetheless, they may reject virtually all governmental regulations on firearms; they may think that the dangers to others are insufficiently substantial to justify governmental constraints on private ownership.

Conversely, someone might think there are compelling reasons why governments should restrict a significant number of people from owning most guns, yet also believe that it would be prudent for some individual George to own a gun because he lives in a especially high-crime area. Someone who holds this view might also think it is morally appropriate for George to own the gun, even if in so doing he violates the law. Although these continua raise morally significant issues, since they do not directly influence the policy debates, I set them aside. I am primarily concerned here with policy. Therefore, I shall say little more about these last two dimensions.

Even when narrowing the focus to competing policies, we have a plethora of options: sets of possible points on the first three dimensions. Attempting to name all of them would be not just confusing but impossible. However, we need not despair. We have a sensible way of narrowing our initial discussion to a more manageable set of policy options. Then, as the inquiry progresses, we can begin to expand our policy horizons. Our first inclination might be to identify two options: each would be a set of points at opposite extremes of the three policy continua. One extreme would be a complete gun ban; the other would place no limitations on who can own any firearm. That strategy would be unproductive since virtually no one holds the extreme on all—and probably not on any—of the policy scales. This illustrates my point: we should stop thinking that the debate is simply whether one supports or opposes gun control. This is more apparent once we notice that although most people tend to embrace positions roughly on the same end of all three scales, others embrace exotic mixtures. For instance, someone might want few weapons available to private citizens, yet want virtually no restrictions on those guns that people can permissibly own, while others may prefer making most guns available to virtually everyone, but want serious restrictions of guns people can privately own.

Once we move beyond the limited view that there are just two options, we see that the policy debates center on three questions: *Who* can own *which guns*, and *in what ways*? Since I cannot identify, let alone definitively discuss, every option, I focus the investigation by employing three simplifying locutions that capture the most common *broad* options.

1. Those who think we should permit most people to own many types of firearms, and want few restrictions on their acquisition, transfer, use, and storage, advocate a *serious claim to bear arms*. In many advocates' views, this claim is a right. However, I use this wording to leave open the option that people may have a legitimate claim to own gun, even if the claim is not, properly speaking, a right.

2. Those who think we should deny many classes of people the legal authority to own many types of firearms, and want to substantially restrict the transfer, use, and storage of those firearms available to them, I deem *serious gun control* advocates.

3. Those embracing options between these views, albeit usually somewhat closer to the second, are *moderate gun control* advocates. Proponents of this option will prohibit some people from owning some types of guns, and support minor restrictions on that ownership. People in this third camp usually oppose extensive or highly intrusive restrictions, even as they support more significant gun control than that advocated by groups such as the NRA.

These simplifications mask important disagreements among advocates of various alternatives. However, it will be beneficial to use these locutions when initially explaining and evaluating the armchair, rights-based, and empirical arguments.

Before I can profitably discuss the policy arguments beginning in chapter 2, I provide a brief history of firearms. This history is far from exhaustive. Although fascinating, much of the history is tangential to the current inquiry. Nonetheless, it is important that we have a broad understanding of who invented firearms; who, when, why, and how they were refined; and who used them, in what circumstances, and in what ways. Although understanding what drove their development, refinement, and deployment will not straightforwardly resolve the moral issues, it will inform them. It helps us better understand the nature and purpose of firearms. It also helps explain why there are so many privately owned guns in the United States, and why the issue of the private ownership of guns is so important to a significant minority of Americans.

THE HISTORY OF FIREARMS

We can begin to understand these issues by exploring an overarching historical question: Why were firearms discovered in one part of the world yet became more commonly used, refined, and manufactured elsewhere? In answering this question, we can begin to isolate the nature and value of firearms while explaining their unique historical role in U.S. history.

The story starts in China where gunpowder, and eventually firearms, were developed sometime in the ninth century AD (Needham, J. 1985: 6). For several hundred years, China was the only country that had them. However, by the early 1200s, as Chinese trade expanded into the West, firearms were found in India, Europe, and parts of the Middle East. For reasons I explain later, they were generally more useful in some of these environments. Soon thereafter, early firearms—in those days that meant primarily cannon—came to be principally developed, refined, manufactured, and used in Europe (Buchanan, B. J. 2006: 3–4; Chase, K. 2003: 2).

Their Military Uses

For at least half a millennium, the only uses of firearms were military. They had no other obvious function. Indeed, during these early centuries, they were not even especially effective military weapons. Their flaws were substantial, pervasive, and obvious. Cannon took a long time to load and fire, were dangerous to use, difficult to move, and inaccurate (Chase, K. 2003). It could take up to an hour to load and shoot them; they were so unsafe that the gunners "risked being blown up each time they applied the match" (Chase, K. 2003: 23). They were extremely heavy and therefore difficult to transport and to place so that they faced the desired target. Finally, even when they worked, they were wildly inaccurate. Initially, their primary use may well have been simply to scare the enemy.

Because of these limitations, cannon were offensively and defensively useful only in environments where speed and accuracy were not essential. Thus, they could be useful if an army had the ability and time to aim them toward an important fixed target, and if the target was sufficiently large so that it did not matter exactly where the cannon ball struck it. Armies could also use them against infantry that attacked in wide straight lines. In those circumstances, it did not matter that the cannon ball veered significantly off course. It could still down a number of enemy soldiers even if they were not the soldiers at which the cannoneer had aimed.

Given these limitations, cannon (and later muskets) were ineffective if used by or against nomadic peoples like the Mongols and many Arabic tribes. The nomads could not use cannon offensively since they lacked the wherewithal to transport them long distances. They had no need for them defensively since they had few fixed sites requiring defense.

Countries whose most common enemies were nomadic, likewise, had no reason to use cannon against them. China could not use them offensively since the Mongols did not have walled cities vulnerable to siege. China also had no need of them defensively since the Mongols typically attacked on horseback and did not advance in long straight lines. China defended itself by erecting walls. Archers defended the walls to stop soldiers trying to scale them; swordsmen battled soldiers who made it to the top.

Cannon's demonstrable limitations were not a significant hindrance in Western Europe where citizens were non-nomadic, their armies were less mobile, and their most common enemies lived in walled cities. In this environment, cannon were militarily valuable. They were effective weapons offensively if one's army was attacking an opponent's city. Because of the cannon ball's trajectory, it was better able to breach city walls than boulders launched by catapults. Defensively, they were effective when placed atop city walls where residents could use them to repel invading armies. Since their cannon were elevated relative to the adjoining land, the cannon balls could go farther than those fired by the invaders. In sum, within this environment and battling these enemies, firearms had an important, albeit limited, military role.

A century or so later, after armies learned how to mount cannon on ships—where their weight was not a military impediment—they discovered new and effective uses for them. Mounted cannon were valuable when battling other countries' warships; they were also effective when attacking their adversaries' seaside towns. Especially on smaller, more maneuverable ships, the captain could relatively quickly "aim" the cannon and "move" it within striking range (Chase, K. 2003: 24, 71). Of course, cannon were still notoriously inaccurate. However, when shooting at a large ship or an entire town, this was not a serious military limitation.

This brief history of early firearms reveals a basic fact about them. From their infancy, all uses were military and all efforts to improve them sought to make them more effective militarily. Developers strove to make them quicker, lighter, more accurate, and more powerful; in short, they sought to make them more effective at besting enemies.

What was true of cannon was also true of long guns and, still later, pistols. Long guns were essentially cannon writ small. The mechanisms were the same. The uses were the same. Their weaknesses were the same. Early muskets used a "matchlock" to ignite the powder and propel the musket ball out the barrel. Soldiers had to light the musket's fuse, just as a cannoneer had to light a cannon's fuse. Because of the matchlock's volatility, an infantryman had to be cautious to prevent the gunpowder from exploding in his hands. Moreover, just as cannon were not useful by or against nomadic people, muskets were likewise "completely useless" for and against nomads (Chase, K. 2003: 24). They were also useless to nomads. Their soldiers could not load them, aim them, light their fuses, or fire them while riding on horseback. That is why nomadic armies continued to rely on the bow and arrow centuries after firearms were developed. In the hands of accomplished archers, these weapons were quieter, lighter, quicker, and more accurate than muskets. Soldiers could also wield them while on horseback.

Even in environments like Western Europe where long guns had some military purpose, their use was limited. Cavalry could not use a musket since they could not load or fire them while on horseback. Only infantry could employ them; they were not especially useful even to them. Not only were they slow and difficult to master, until the early 1700s, most muskets were so inaccurate that the musket ball could veer five feet off target while traveling 200 feet (Chase, K. 2003: 25). Doubtless that is why, well into the 1700s, most infantry regiments deployed more pikemen (soldiers carrying long pointed pikes) than musketeers. It was not until the end of the century that the standard infantry unit would have as many musketeers as pikemen. Musketeers did not replace pikemen until muskets were further refined: until they became safer, quicker, more accurate, *and* were fitted with bayonets. This last feature allowed infantry to combine two military roles. When the muskets could not fire, for example, in rainy weather, the soldiers could still use their bayonets. Finally, by the time of the American Revolution, muskets had become the most common (but not only) military weapon (Chase, K. 2003: 56–60, 62). Even so, it was decades before they became sufficiently accurate and reliable to be clearly more advantageous than the pike or the bow for the common soldier (Kyle, C. and Doyle, W. 2013: 198).

Indeed, it was not until the 1800s—nearly a millennium after firearms were first developed—before muskets were as accurate in the hands of an infantryman as bows were in the hands of an accomplished archer (Chase, K. 2003: 27). So why did armies use them earlier despite their limitations? By the 1700s, they had one significant advantage. A new recruit could become reasonably adept with a musket quickly; learning to wield a bow effectively was far more time-consuming. Despite this advantage, muskets still had problems, especially in rainy weather. The introduction of the percussion cap in the early 1800s overcame this limitation. Soldiers no longer needed a visible spark to light the powder. Nonetheless, each bullet still had to be loaded manually. Thus, although they were faster than the old matchlock, they were slower than a bow in the hands of a skilled archer.

In the following decades, refinements of long guns occurred more quickly. Each change made them more accurate, faster, or more reliable. These developments made firearms more deadly, and thus, essential for most military engagements. The final significant development came in the last half of the 1800s with the refinement and widespread manufacture of the self-contained cartridge. These cartridges included all the required mechanisms for igniting the powder and propelling the bullet. This made the modern long gun an indispensable weapon for the average soldier. Soldiers no longer needed a knife, sword, a bow, or a pike. Consequently, except in rare circumstances (where stealth was required), these weapons were consigned to the dustbin of military history.

Although all innovations began in response to military demands (Kyle, C. and Doyle, W. 2013: 2254), these developments paved the way for more extensive use of firearms by civilians, at least in advantageous environments.

Their Expanded Use by Civilians

These abovementioned technological limitations and historical/sociological factors explain why for many years so few private citizens had any interest in having guns. Prior to the mid-1600s, there were no important civilian uses for them. They were unsuitable for hunting, defense, or committing a crime. The matchlock was just too slow and too inaccurate. Once the flintlock was developed, long guns did have some civilian uses. Even so, they were far from satisfactory. Although faster and less dangerous than its predecessors, it was still slow. Moreover, they were so expensive that few ordinary people could afford them.

Even after they were improved between the late 1700s and the mid-1800s, few Europeans wanted a firearm. These people lived in urban, largely secure communities. They grew up in homes where their parents had no need for firearms; their children could not see a compelling reason to acquire them. In contrast, many American civilians were familiar with firearms because in *their* environment guns had more—and more important—uses. Many rural folks used them for hunting to feed themselves and their families. They used them to kill pests that ravaged their crops and animals that preyed on their livestock. Moreover, rural people often lived miles from police and even neighbors; firearms were the primary form of self-defense. Finally, after 1865 many American civilians had firearms because after the Civil War, the government permitted soldiers in both armies to keep their weapons. This dramatically increased private gun ownership in the United States (Kyle, C. and Doyle, W. 2013: 870).

Of course, the same features that made the new, improved firearms more suitable for hunting and self-defense also made them effective offensive weapons. Criminals sought both long guns and pistols; they became the preferred weapons of bank and train robbers. They later became especially valuable to organized crime. Gun manufacturers originally developed the Thompson submachine gun for use by American troops in World War I. However, these weapons were ready for mass production too late for widespread deployment during the war. After the war, there was a glut of them. Organized crime obtained and used many of them during and following Prohibition (Kyle, C. and Doyle, W. 2013: 1959–99).

WHAT THIS HISTORY HELPS EXPLAIN

There are three critical insights we should draw from this history.

They Are All Firearms

All firearms spring from the same scientific, technological, and military lineage. All rely on the same scientific principles; all have the same basic purpose; all have the same primary use. This fact is affirmed in Chase's authoritative history of firearms that starts with cannons, explains how they morphed into muskets, and then much later how they led to the development of modern-day rifles and pistols (Chase, K. 2003).

The point seems so obvious that it does not merit mention. However, we need to understand their technological kinship. It rests at the core of the debate about the second policy continuum: Which types of firearms should we allow (some) citizens to privately own? Understanding firearms' common lineage acknowledges that they are all lethal weapons, although the degree of their lethality differs. People with bazookas and howitzers can kill more people more quickly than they can with .22 caliber rifles. However, they are all weapons designed to be lethal. The rationale for treating the former differently from the latter is not that the latter are firearms while the former are not. The rationale is simply that it is riskier to let private citizens own the former types of firearms.

They Are Inherently Dangerous to Possess

The second lesson is implied by the first. Their history demonstrates that owning firearms of *any* type is an inherently dangerous activity, even though owning some types is riskier than owning others. Although owning them is dangerous, that does not automatically show that we should not permit citizens to have them or that it is imprudent or immoral for people to own them. It does indicate that we cannot intelligently decide whether or how to permit or constrain this activity until we understand just how risky they are.

That owning firearms is inherently dangerous is evident given their history, which reveals their nature, development, and use. From the 800s until the 1700s, their only function was military. They were developed to threaten and perpetrate harm. What other function could cannon have had? When developers worked to improve them, they changed them to overcome early weapons' limitations. They worked to make cannon faster, safer, more mobile, more accurate, or more powerful—and preferably all the above. Centuries later, manufacturers made similar changes in long guns; all changes were meant to make firearms more useful and more lethal. For instance, they would permit a soldier to kill an enemy from a distance even if the enemy were wearing armor. The purposes for developing and refining them is evident throughout their history, not only as recounted by traditional historians (Buchanan, B. J. 1996, 2006; Chase, K. 2003) but also by strong pro-gun advocates (Kyle, C. and Doyle, W. 2013).

Historians focused mainly on cannon and their role in military conflict. The pro-gun advocates focused primarily on the history of long guns and pistols. Both sources provide a consistent story: long guns were developed and deployed late in the history of firearms. Handguns came even later. Early pistols were plagued not only with the problems besetting muskets, they had unique ones that persisted well into the 1800s. It was not until the American Civil War that pistols became relatively dependable and more accurate. Even during that war, only officers standardly had pistols. It was not until after that war—with the development of the Colt 45—that handguns became far more user-friendly and cheaper, and thus, more useful both in the military and for the average private citizen (Kyle, C. and Doyle, W. 2013: chap. 3).

The history of firearms shows why possessing them is inherently dangerous in ways that owning other objects sometimes used as weapons (knives, machetes, baseball bats, and tire irons) are not. Although some people may use these latter objects as weapons, they were not designed as weapons. People created, used, and refined these objects for nonviolent ends. When automakers improved tire irons, they were not trying to make them more lethal. They wanted to provide owners a lighter and stronger tool for removing a wheel's lug nuts. Blacksmiths improved machetes by making them lighter, stronger, and sharper and thus, easier to wield when cutting dense undergrowth. Of course these improvements also made machetes more lethal. However, that was not the aim of these improvements. In contrast, when gunsmiths altered firearms, they did so to make them more effective weapons. That is the core aim of firearms. All other uses ride piggyback on the violent one.

Of course, in saying that possessing firearms is inherently dangerous is not to claim that firearms are agents. No one has ever said, thought, or believed that. What *is* meant in saying that owning them is inherently dangerous is to say that given their design, they are more likely to be used to cause harm, more likely to cause harm accidentally, and more likely to lead to death when used in an attempted suicide. Any nefarious use of them arises from their central character. Put differently, to say that owning them is inherently dangerous is to say that owning them is dangerous in ways that owning chemical and biological weapons is, and in ways that owning tire irons and baseball bats is not. Possessing the former makes it decidedly easier for agents to cause significant harm, either intentionally or unintentionally, while possessing the latter does not. People are more likely to cause harm with guns than with ballpoint pens, Q-tips, or butter knives, although, of course, in some hands, these latter implements *can* be weapons.

Explaining Their Special Role in US History

Three, their history helps explain why and how guns played a central role in US history, a role they did not play in any other developed country. This central historical role helps explain why US citizens' interest in owning guns is so much higher than in other modern, industrial, developed countries; it explains why its citizens are more resistant to serious gun control.

Five distinct, but somewhat intermingled, historical influences converged to create and sustain many Americans' interest in, attachment to, and a belief in the importance of the private ownership of guns. All these influences are partly a function of timing.

One, the United States' first century coincided with a period of significant improvements in and the wider accessibility of firearms. For eight centuries, firearms were generally slow, heavy, dangerous to use, inaccurate, unreliable, and expensive. In less than 200 years—from the time of the early colonists through the westward expansion—firearms became safer, more reliable, faster, more accurate, more powerful, and cheaper. This quirk of timing made US citizens far more comfortable with and dependent on firearms than were comparable citizens of any other developed country. As the next four factors reveal, these improved firearms defined key elements of US development in ways unlike that of any other Westernized country. Therefore, it is not surprising that its citizens were more drawn to firearms, more likely to own them, more likely to use them, and more likely to resist efforts to control private ownership of them.

Two, guns played unique military roles in US history. The country had its origins, won independence, and became a more significant world power in an era in which firearms were demonstrably more advantageous than they had been at similar developmental stages of industrialized European countries. Among other things, the US did not always have a professionalized army. In its early years, it relied heavily on private citizens to man its militia.

Three, owning guns played vital roles for many US citizens. The same was not true for citizens in most industrialized countries. By the early 1800s, most Europeans lived in states with established armies; half their citizens resided in urban areas with established police forces. They had become accustomed to life without firearms; they saw no compelling reason to acquire them. In contrast, most Americans (90%) lived in small towns or sparsely populated rural areas where there were few or no police (Stevenson, K. 2013). Many of these people were farmers with few neighbors. They thought they needed firearms to defend themselves, to hunt game, and to protect their crops and livestock from pests and predators. In this environment, guns were, at least, advantageous and arguably necessary.

Four, more Americans owned guns. Many people wanted them for both civilian and military reasons. Since they had become cheaper, more Americans could afford them. Moreover, as I mentioned earlier, at the end of the Civil War, the government permitted soldiers on both sides of the conflict to keep their government-issued weapons. This led to a noticeable spike in the number of privately owned firearms (Kyle, C. and Doyle, W. 2013: 869).

Five, guns were the primary engine of the rapid expansion westward. The 1865 call by Horace Greely to "Go West, young man," occurred just as guns become plentiful, reliable, fast, and relatively cheap. Many adventurous or poor Americans, dissatisfied with life in the East and yearning for promised wealth in the West, were convinced to heed Greely's plea. Virtually all went armed. Although some of the US western expansion was enabled by land purchases from other Western powers—for example, the Louisiana Purchase in 1803—most were achieved at the end of a gun.

It was during this era that firearms powered one of the darkest moral stains on American history. Guns gave individual settlers and the federal military the ability to displace, relocate, and slaughter Native Americans. By the early 1800s, Native American Indians populated huge swaths of the central and western parts of the continent. Sometimes settlers expressly attacked the Indians to drive them off the land. In other cases, Indians (who saw the settlers as interlopers) attacked the settlers, who subsequently "defended" themselves . . . and then often went on the offensive. Why, exactly, most settlers thought that it was acceptable for them to displace or kill the native inhabitants, I am unsure. What is clear is that their proclivities were created or reinforced by government policy. The government acted as if the West were unclaimed land that they could give or sell to settlers as they pleased. Given the settlers' superior numbers and firepower, they eventually prevailed. Those Native Americans that survived were consigned to reservations, typically on highly undesirable land (Deloria, V., Jr. 1969). Given this confluence of factors, we can see why the United States has a gun culture unique in the world.

Before proceeding, I note that there are people who explain the United States' unique interest in guns differently. In *Gunning for America*, Haag argues that the core explanation stems from gun manufactures' success in marketing their products. Her core story focuses on the Winchester rifle (Haag, P. 2016). I do not think her claim is bizarre or demonstrably false. Marketing can create and sustain people's desire to purchase a product, even ones they do not need. Nonetheless, although I suspect this is part of the story, I doubt it is the whole or primary part. I am more inclined to think that effective marketing reinforces the explanations proffered here. Even without the marketing, Americans would still have a unique interest in guns.

With these three historical insights to hand, we are better equipped to decide whether people have a serious claim to bear arms and whether we should have moderate or serious gun control. It helps map the terrain we must cross in answering these questions.

THE BOOK'S STRUCTURE

In the remainder of the book, I describe and then evaluate three types of arguments about gun control: armchair arguments, arguments asserting a right to bear arms, and empirical arguments about the costs and benefits of private gun ownership. Each approach addresses, in its own way, the three core questions we must answer: (1) Who should have (2) which guns, and (3) how, if at all, should we regulate the guns people may legitimately own? Although these arguments address the same questions, they approach them differently. Although key considerations may arise in each context, the way to understand and evaluate each argument differs.

Chapter 2 describes and evaluates armchair arguments for and against serious gun control. Armchair arguments are arguments that do not *expressly* employ empirical studies about the benefits and costs of private gun ownership, or the benefits and costs of government's efforts to control private gun ownership. Valuable armchair arguments are not devoid of empirical content. Rather the knowledge that informs them lays in the background, rather than the foreground, of the argument. Of course, some people sometimes advance putative armchair arguments without any awareness of the relevant empirical evidence and sans credible background knowledge. However, that is not normal, let alone ideal.

Although such arguments cannot settle this debate, as I explain more fully in chapter 2, they frame and inform it, and, thus, are essential to its resolution. They establish a burden of proof; that is, they identify which view is most plausible if neither the rights-based nor the empirical arguments are compelling. They shape discussions about a serious right to bear arms. They guide researchers in designing studies about the costs and benefits of owning guns. They give informed people a sensible way of evaluating researchers' findings and inferences from those findings. I argue that the armchair arguments tilt in favor of serious gun control.

In chapters 3 and 4, I discuss versions of the view that individuals have not just a claim but a right to privately own guns. According to advocates, this right is sufficiently strong that it can be overridden, if at all, only if there is (a) overwhelming evidence of the costs of allowing private gun ownership and (b) overwhelming evidence of the benefits of gun control. Shy such evidence, gun control will always be a violation of people's rights and, thus, morally unacceptable.

I divide this discussion to make it more manageable. In chapter 3, I describe common philosophical views about the nature of rights. This helps locate gun advocates' claims for a serious right to bear arms within a broader theoretical framework. I explain why this is primarily a moral debate—a claim about what the law should permit. It is not a debate about the status of the law within the United States or elsewhere. I identify basic distinctions between the types and functions of rights.

In chapter 4, I describe the myriad forms the right to bear arms take. Some advocates claim that we have a fundamental right to own guns. Others claim that we have a fundamental right to security and that the private ownership of guns is an important (and perhaps necessary) means of protecting security. These are the two most common ways in which advocates ground the right and explain why it is extremely stringent. Those making these claims think or hope that by establishing such a right, they can resolve the debate about gun control without having to engage either the armchair arguments or the empirical evidence.

I describe their most common and most plausible arguments for a right. I seek to give the most accurate, fair accounting of their respective views. I seek to identify, and then focus on, themes connecting their disparate views. I then explain why their belief that a claim of right can resolve the gun control debate is mistaken; their hope, misplaced. I isolate dilemmas facing pro-gun advocates, dilemmas that further show that their view is far from compelling. This sets the stage for discussing the empirical evidence.

Before I can assess the available evidence, I want to determine what evidence would help us resolve this issue and how we might obtain it. In chapter 5, I identify obstacles to obtaining evidence and explore possible ways of overcoming those obstacles. Rarely can we straightforwardly read empirical truths from bare numbers. We must know what to look for, how we might find it, and how we should interpret it, especially given what will inevitably be the presence of countervailing data.

In chapter 6, I describe the proffered empirical evidence, first for the benefits of private gun ownership, then purported findings about the costs of private gun ownership. Finally, I explain the agnostic claim that we have little plausible evidence fully supporting either of the previous contentions. Then, in chapter 7, I evaluate said evidence. The empirical evidence at hand is thin, especially since congressional supporters of the NRA have effectively forbidden the Centers for Disease Control and Prevention from conducting or funding empirical studies that might be used to support arguments for gun control (Kellermann, A. et al. 2013). Given these constraints, we are left with suggestive, but less than wholly satisfying, data.

The limitations on empirical evidence make the armchair arguments even more vital to an adequate assessment of the arguments for serious gun control or a serious claim to bear arms. Having set the burden of proof, we now have some idea of how to proceed given the thinness of the empirical evidence.

The difficulty of obtaining detailed and reliable empirical evidence about the costs and benefits of private gun ownership is no reason to avoid seeking evidence. Nor is it a reason not to employ evidence we can obtain. If nothing else, the empirical evidence will inform our armchair arguments.

These considerations set the stage for my positive proposals, laid out in chapter 8. I first explore the potential costs of implementing strong gun control, even if such control is abstractly warranted. These costs must be considered given the number of people who own guns coupled with the strong desire of many of them to privately own them. Making any activity illegal is costly. Making a very popular activity illegal is exceedingly costly. I conclude that this argument, based on an analogy with Prohibition, might furnish reasons to oppose a gun ban, but it does not provide strong reasons against forms of gun control most commonly advocated.

I also briefly mention a series of reasonable gun control measures. Individually they may not significantly limit harm caused by private gun ownership. However, if my arguments throughout the book are plausible, collectively these measures should be highly beneficial; moreover, most are compatible with the most sensible arguments for a right to bear arms.

Finally, I conclude that even if, at every turn, we interpret the evidence favorably for gun advocates, gun owners should at least take moral and legal responsibility for harm caused—intentionally or unintentionally—by the guns they own. Thus, they should be required to carry liability insurance to compensate for such harm. There is good reason to make gun owners strictly liable for any harm that results from their owning firearms.

Chapter 2

Armchair Arguments

To evaluate arguments for or against gun control we must begin with a careful development and assessment of the respective armchair arguments. Some will think this assertion is at least misguided and probably flat-out wrong. The response is understandable since this is a case where it seems rights-based arguments or empirical evidence should rule the argumentative roost. The perception is exacerbated by the fact that here—as elsewhere—disputants sometimes resort to wildly implausible armchair (or "common sense") arguments. Frequent abuse of these arguments gives all such arguments a bad name. That is unfortunate. Despite the importance of rights-based and empirical evidence and a raft of rotten armchair arguments, rejecting all the latter is a significant mistake. It is not simply that we must tolerate informed armchair arguments; such arguments are essential for good reasoning about this, and, indeed most, topics political and moral.

To understand why, we must first be clear about what we mean by "armchair arguments" and then explain how to distinguish wildly implausible ones from informed ones. These arguments are not solely about people's rights nor do they *expressly* appeal to studies or statistics. However, that does not mean that plausible ones run free of empirical evidence. It means the empirical elements of the reasoning lay in the background rather than the foreground. Compelling armchair arguments are supported by robust background knowledge of science, history, politics, and human behavior. Observant, thoughtful, and broadly educated people have reservoirs of information, an arsenal of reasoning skills, and guiding intellectual traits (curiosity, intellectual honesty, skepticism, and self-criticism) that guide their understanding and evaluation of most decisions, including those about controversial public policies. The problem, however, is that although there is an important distinction between implausible and reasonable armchair arguments, we sometimes have difficulty distinguishing them, at least if we are not cautious and scrupulously honest when scrutinizing them. Some armchair arguments that initially seem implausible may, upon closer examination, be quite compelling, while some that initially appear plausible may, upon closer examination, be vulnerable to devastating criticisms.

I begin by examining armchair arguments that play a prominent role in many popular debates over gun control. Some of these flirt with the language of rights; others have the ring of ersatz empirical arguments. Even if these arguments are not ultimately plausible, most have rhetorical power: they persuade some number of people engaged in this debate. That is reason enough to examine them carefully. Furthermore, as we shall see, even ones that are less than convincing frequently contain hints of more substantial insights and arguments. An analysis of these arguments will set the stage for (a) more sophisticated philosophical arguments for a right to bear arms—addressed extensively in the following two chapters—and for (b) empirically based arguments about the benefits and costs of permitting private ownership of guns, which I address in chapters 6 and 7.

Although rigorous armchair arguments are individually insufficient to support a definitive conclusion on this complex policy, collectively they play four significant roles in assessing these proposed policies.

THE NATURE AND ROLE OF ARMCHAIR ARGUMENTS

Their Roles

Armchair arguments are essential to resolving complex policy issues. They play four vital roles. First, they help set the evidentiary burden of proof by determining what the preponderance of armchair evidence shows. In so doing, they indicate how we should resolve an issue when the rights-based arguments are insufficiently compelling and the empirical evidence is unavailable, flimsy, unclear, or conflicting. When these other arguments fail, we need not throw up our hands in despair. Sometimes circumstances demand that we must act even if we have less than overwhelming evidence. Occasionally we should just stand pat with our current practices, although we should remember that in doing so we are still doing something, namely, we are reinforcing the status quo. Sometimes that is acceptable; sometimes it is not.

In short, understanding where the burden of proof rests may guide us in resolving some complex public policy debates. Exactly how these arguments play this role will become more apparent as we explore several armchair arguments in the next major section of this chapter, as well as others that emerge in later chapters. I do not contend that burden of proof arguments always play a significant—let alone determinative—role in policy debates. Sometimes there is not even enough background knowledge to give us any guidance about where to place that burden. However, that does not happen always and probably not often.

Second, armchair arguments provide background information that shapes our understanding and evaluation of arguments for a right to bear arms. Rights-based arguments often rely on claims about people's interests, motivations, and behavior—claims often undergirded by armchair arguments.

Third, armchair arguments are essential for generating and shaping scientifically testable hypotheses about the respective costs and benefits of gun control. Plausible hypotheses about the private ownership of guns are formed and informed by what we know, what we know that we don't know, what we need to know to make a reasonable decision, and a sense of how we might obtain the required information. If you want to understand why your car won't start, you construct hypotheses. Any plausible ones must be based on knowledge about the way cars work, in particular, about the way cars start. A four-year-old wouldn't have a clue how to construct a hypothesis since she wouldn't have a clue about what might explain the car's failure. The more you know about cars, the more likely you are to frame a testable hypothesis and identify why it won't start. You might speculate that the battery has lost its charge, and if so, venture that it did so because the battery is worn out, the car's alternator is defective, or the alternator belt is loose. You might subsequently test each option, starting with the most likely one. If none of those pan out, you might check to see if the starter or solenoid is defective or if the wires running to either are loose.

However, you would not examine the floor mats to see if they were clean or if the rear window was foggy or if the driver's seat was torn. Why not? Because you cannot think of any plausible reason how any of these factors would interfere with the car's starting. Of course, you might be mistaken in casually dismissing these options. We may be insufficiently imaginative, or we may have limited knowledge of the design of newer cars. Perhaps some newer cars are designed so that they will not start if the driver's seat is empty. In such cars, a torn seat may be "interpreted" as indicating that the seat is empty, and therefore, blocks the car from starting. What this fictional example illustrates is that only someone who understands car mechanics is likely to identify the cause of the car's not starting. The point is not just idle curiosity. If someone can isolate the cause of its not starting, then she is more likely to know how to fix it.

Likewise, an astute family physician with deep reservoirs of biological, chemical, and medical knowledge is more likely to correctly diagnose the causes of a patient's skin rash, fast heartbeat, or the inability to raise her right arm. Even if the physician cannot make a firm diagnosis, she would have sufficient background information to determine which tests to order to narrow the possibilities. Barring bizarre circumstances, she will not order a leg x-ray to determine why the person has a rash or examine between the patient's toes to ascertain why she has a fast heartbeat. A well-trained and experienced physician knows that these factors are unlikely to cause any of the aforementioned symptoms. That shows why background knowledge is so important in framing hypotheses (making tentative diagnoses), designing or ordering tests, and making inferences from those test. The entire process starts with the doctor making informed armchair diagnoses grounded in a vast storehouse of medical, physiological, and psychological knowledge.

Four, armchair arguments play a central role in evaluating experiments to test a hypothesis. Sometimes these arguments should make us cautious before we jump to a conclusion based on the experiment's results. The car mechanic may not immediately conclude that the problem is a failing alternator simply because a test shows that the alternator is not currently generating sufficient voltage to recharge the battery. Why? Because that test may not fit well with other reported symptoms—for example, that the air conditioning is not cooling the car's interior. The combination of symptoms might indicate that the car's universal belt—one that charges the alternator *and* runs the air conditioner's compressor—is loose. The physician may be cautious in how she interprets a low white blood cell count if her first impression (an autoimmune disorder) does not fit with other reported symptoms, say, lower back pain or blurry vision, or if it is inconsistent with the patient's most recent blood work. Experimental findings should be evaluated in light of informed background knowledge.

Armchair arguments play a similar role when considering and assessing proposed public policies. They help place the burden of proof; they inform and help evaluate rights-based arguments; they shape viable hypotheses and help researchers design studies to confirm or falsify those hypotheses; they give us an informed perspective from which to evaluate studies' findings. I explore the first role here and then again in the final chapter. I explore the second role in chapters 3 and 4. I elucidate the third and fourth roles later in this chapter. I then illustrate how these function in the gun control debate when, in chapters 5 through 7, I discuss and evaluate empirical research about the costs and benefits of private gun ownership.

A Caution

Although armchair arguments are essential, they are insufficient to establish firm conclusions about gun control. One persistent worry about them is that their premises—the background "knowledge" informing them—may be unreliable and can lead us astray. Even highly plausible background information is sometimes erroneous. The history of humankind is littered with instances where smart, thoughtful people embraced, and acted upon, false beliefs or half-truths. At the time people held them, many of these beliefs seemed highly plausible, even nigh-on indubitable. Throughout the Middle Ages, most people—including most learned members of society— were convinced that the earth was the center of the universe. Until the 1800s, no one knew about germs; hence, most "physicians" and scientists assumed illnesses had other causes, for example, "bad humours" or demonic possession. Such mistakes did not magically vanish in the twentieth century. For decades physicians assumed that stress and spicy foods caused stomach ulcers. Two Australian doctors rejected this common—indeed settled—belief and argued that most ulcers were caused by a bacterium, *H. pylori* (*Helicobacter pylori*). Initially the medical community scoffed at these Aussies' proposal. The researchers persisted; eventually their evidence convinced the medical community that its deeply held belief was false. Most ulcers can be treated with one course of the appropriate antibiotic. Patients did not have to endure ulcers or simply try to mask their symptoms by taking assorted antacids.

Moreover, many beliefs we now take for granted were ones our predecessors not only did not hold, they had no reason to hold. Why should they have believed that diets high in trans fats would significantly increase people's chance of developing heart disease? They did not even know what trans fats were, let alone how they could lead to heart disease. Or why should they have believed that lead in gasoline and in paint would diminish the intelligence and self-control of those exposed to this metal? In both cases, the causal explanations are far from obvious. Without more sophisticated chemical and metabolic knowledge, the links between these substances and human diseases are not only not obvious, they are wholly mysterious. Yet both claims are true and are now considered uncontroversial.

This knowledge should not lead us to jettison armchair arguments; however, it should remind us that we are fallible creatures with flawed investigatory and reasoning skills. Awareness of our limitations should make us more cautious when assessing controversial policies. We must remember that although background knowledge is essential to understanding and assessing new data and potential public policies, even the beliefs about which we are most certain may be false. Therefore, rationality dictates that we must be skeptical and open minded. That said, circumstances often demand that we act, even when we have less than unshakeable evidence. We must work with the information we have.

ARMCHAIR ARGUMENTS AGAINST GUN CONTROL

Although advocates of a serious claim to bear arms offer some positive arguments for their claims, they usually begin by trying to rebut arguments for serious gun control. Gun advocates plausibly think the initial burden of proof rests on advocates for serious gun control. They believe, therefore, that if they can undermine arguments for control, then they have effectively shown that people have a serious claim to bear arms. (As I noted earlier, many construe this claim as a right.) I follow their lead: I first discuss armchair arguments against serious gun control before discussing the positive armchair arguments for a serious claim to bear arms.

Why Control Any Guns?

Gun advocates often pose a plausible opening question: Why, out of all the manmade objects in our world, should we control the private ownership of guns? We do not prohibit all people from owning, limit any subclass of people from owning, or (generally) prescribe how someone must store a stove, a baby crib, or a bottle of shampoo. We would scoff at someone who seriously advocated stove, crib, or shampoo control. This shows why the initial burden of proof rests on gun control advocates: there must be a good reason for controlling the ownership and use of any inanimate object. If there were no such reason, then the laws and regulations would be pointless and unacceptably intrusive.

Unfortunately, this quick answer is too quick. We *do* control the aforementioned objects to some degree or in some circumstances. We have policies requiring stoves to contain sufficient fire-retardant insulation so that their ordinary use does not cause fires in surrounding cabinetry or walls. We have rules limiting the distance between slats in baby cribs to diminish the chance that an infant will be strangled by getting her head caught between slats. We have rules governing the production of shampoos to ensure that their use does not damage the user's scalp, skin, or eyes. The government requires evidence of the quality of some products' construction; it often requires that an object's safety be demonstrated before they are sold.

The government also restricts how and when some objects are used, say, when and how fireworks are publicly displayed. It prohibits passengers from carrying four ounces (or more) of shampoo or lotion onto an airplane. The Food and Drug Administration requires prescription medications to be rigorously tested before they are prescribed to patients. Most of us are quite happy that the government fulfills these roles. We are incensed if we or someone we love is harmed or killed because the government fails to protect us. Of course, we may find some regulations inconvenient or annoying or misguided. However, we think this is a valuable governmental role that *generally* makes us safer.

In sum, governments control the construction, distribution, use, and ownership of many inanimate objects, even if we do not initially describe their restrictions in that way. Usually we simply claim that they establish regulations to protect citizens' safety. That is also the core purpose of gun control measures.

Does this common rationale give us legitimate reasons to control guns? Should firearms be subject to more extensive controls than deodorant, peanut butter, and soup spoons? It is plausible to think so. Although the earlier arguments suggested that gun control advocates bear the initial burden of proof, these considerations show that this is an epistemological burden government officials frequently meet. The government is morally justified in prohibiting all citizens from owning some objects (live smallpox or nuclear weapons), in prohibiting some classes of people (children under five years of age or people with advanced Alzheimer's) from having or using some objects (automobiles or steam rollers), in prescribing how other objects (antibiotics and narcotics) are obtained, and specifying how still others (hydrochloric acid) must be stored and transported. All these limitations are instituted to protect innocent people from harm.

A gun control advocate could combine this public health approach with the historical argument in the previous chapter to explain why controlling guns is not just something we should consider, it is likely something we should do. Permitting some people to own some guns without restrictions is dangerous in ways and to degrees that allowing people to own toothpaste, tahini, and tape is not. This indicates that the control advocates have met the initial burden of proof; the burden has now shifted to advocates of a serious claim to bear arms.

Gun advocates could claim, however, that although these considerations might give us compelling reasons for stopping a violent former felon or someone who is mentally unstable from having a gun (options on the first continua identified in chapter 1), why should we restrict someone who has never received so much as a parking ticket? Gun control advocates have a plausible response: if owning some item (e.g., the smallpox virus) is very risky, arguably no private citizen should be permitted to have it; it matters not that these people were previously law-abiding. If owning the object is less risky (a bazooka, an assault weapon, or even a handgun), we should still be concerned that some previously law-abiding people will, in some circumstances, intentionally, maliciously, spontaneously, or accidentally misuse the item. When people are stressed, exhausted, ill, depressed, unfocused, jealous, or angry, they often act in ways they would never act in moments of cool reflection. Really good people can do really horrendous actions (LaFollette, H. 2017). The combination of the inherent dangerousness of permitting the private ownership of guns coupled with the aforementioned familiar facts about human behavior, gives us good reason to seriously consider various controls. Whether these factors are sufficient to justify more than minimal gun control depends on three things: (1) Is merely owning a risky object a significant reason to control it? (2) Just how risky is owning guns (more than baking soda but less than smallpox)? (3) Are the benefits of private gun ownership sufficient to override the costs of permitting this risky behavior? The last two questions are familiar features of the gun control debate; we discuss them briefly later in this chapter and again extensively in the chapters 5 through 7. The first is also vital; I briefly explain the issue here and then discuss a variation on it in the final chapter.

One prominent philosopher has argued that criminalizing risky actions is almost always unwarranted (Husak, D. 2008). Even those of us who have misgivings about his stance acknowledge that he isolates something we should remember: making an action illegal *always* has personal and social costs; sometimes these are significant. It costs the state money to police, apprehend, investigate, and punish violators. That is money the government could spend on education or roads or medical care or national parks. Being punished costs individuals who are convicted (or take a plea bargain). Even indisputably just laws, for example, laws against murder, have significant costs. By making an action illegal, we empower police to investigate and interrogate potential suspects; we permit prosecutors to charge those they think are guilty (based on the police's findings), and we permit the state to punish those that judges or juries find guilty. In the process, innocent people may be convicted and sentenced. Even when innocent people are acquitted, they are interrogated, investigated, and charged. The financial and personal costs of enduring the process can be devastating (see Frank Ritter's report on the trial of Clay Shaw in Seigenthaler, J., et al. 1971).

The cost of enforcement is particularly high when the state criminalizes a popular practice. One, it may be expensive—or even impossible—to police the activity, as the United States discovered after prohibiting the sale of alcohol. Even if it *can* be policed, it is costly to investigate, prosecute, and punish violators. Consider the enormous expense of the US War on Drugs, a cost that led some prominent conservatives to eventually support legalization (Buckley, W. F., Jr. 2002/1996). Two, even if the law succeeds in eliminating or controlling usage, it may thereby diminish citizens' respect for the law. This can happen even if the law is wholly reasonable.

Many Southerners resisted racial integration of public schools and public facilities (bathrooms, water fountains, and public transportation). Although segregation was a moral outrage, the battle between the federal government and those opposing integration was exceedingly contentious; some Southerners continue to be hostile toward the federal government sixty years later. The segregationists' animus toward the government has moral ripple effects that still hamstring important governmental programs, including some attempts to promote public health, to protect public safety, and to preserve the environment. That animus undergirds substantial distrust of many government programs.

These examples show why the costs of implementing even wholly warranted gun control policies might be unacceptably high. This gives us a reason to move slowly before implementing gun control. However, we have one reason to think this consideration may have lost some of its bite: fewer Americans own guns than in the past. In 1970, half of all Americans owned guns; by 2012, that number had dropped to 34% (Tavernise, S. and Gebeloff, R. 2013). However, evidence suggests that those who do own guns have an especially intense desire to own them. So the argument from the cost of enforcing serious gun control is still relevant, albeit in different form. It should give ardent gun control advocates some pause.

In sum, these armchair arguments suggest that in countries like the United States with a long history of gun ownership and gun use, the costs of significant gun control would likely be high. Therefore, advocates of serious or stringent (and perhaps even moderate) gun control still seem to carry the burden of proof. That is, gun control advocates must show that the benefits of control are sufficiently high that they outweigh these practical and enforcement costs. These considerations set the stage for five positive arguments for a serious claim to privately own firearms.

Positive Arguments for a Serious Claim to Own Guns

There are five armchair arguments for a serious claim to own guns. The first four construe the claim as a right. The first of these four aver that the right is fundamental.

1. Competent adults have a fundamental right that can be overridden, if at all, only if the costs of granting the right are substantial and its benefits small.

The next three arguments claim people have a derivative right to own a gun. Although the right is not fundamental, it is still morally weighty.

2. The first of these derivative rights is grounded in the general right to be free. One should be able to do what one wants, as long as one does not directly harm another. If one wants to own a gun, she should be able to, unless the costs of doing so are enormous and the benefits relatively small.

3. The second form is grounded in a right to security: in certain environments citizens must own a gun to protect themselves and others. Many think it is insufficient to simply permit people to own a gun. Citizens must be able to carry their weapons—either openly or concealed—when they leave home.

4. The final form of a derivative right is grounded in a right to protect oneself from tyrannical—or potentially tyrannical—governments.

The fifth asserts that citizens have a serious claim to own guns, even if the claim is not a right.

5. Since the benefits of private gun ownership are substantial, and the costs few, then people have a serious claim to own guns, even if they do not, properly speaking, have a right to do so.

All these are sometimes framed as armchair arguments. However, since the first four most commonly feature in the philosophical literature, I *primarily* discuss them in chapters 3 and 4. The fifth best reflects empirical arguments for a serious claim to bear arms. I elucidate and evaluate various incarnations of that argument in chapters 5 through 7. In the current chapter, I focus on arguments from security since these are commonly used armchair arguments for a serious claim to bear arms. These claims are at the core of the third argument; concern for security is also implicit in the chapters on the empirical evidence. After discussing the armchair versions of this argument shortly, I re-engage these concerns again, albeit in different forms, throughout the remainder of the book.

The Need for Security

None of us wants to be robbed, assaulted, or murdered. Many armchair pro-gun arguments aver that guns are an important, and perhaps essential, means of protecting ourselves from attack. Although arguments for security take different forms and deploy different moral reasoning, all spring from the following observations. One of a state's most important jobs is to protect private citizens. It does that by criminalizing attacks on individual citizens. These laws permit police to directly protect citizens from assaults or murder; they empower the police to investigate attacks that do occur; and they enable the relevant legal officials to prosecute and punish offenders. Most people believe that the threat of punishment deters some who would otherwise harm others. In this way the state indirectly protects people's safety.

However, it is generally better to prevent a wrong from occurring than to punish the offender after she caused harm. Gun advocates claim that owning a gun is an important—sometimes a necessary—means of achieving this aim. Guns can protect people in three ways.

SELF-PROTECTION

Suppose Jones plans to attack Smith. If Smith is armed, he may be able to avert the attack by brandishing a gun. If that does not succeed, he may be able to prevent harm by shooting Jones before the attack occurs, or at least before the attack is completed. It seems evident that armed potential victims can sometimes prevent harm, either in their homes or if they are carrying a firearm in public. It is implausible to think that this is not sometimes true. When it does happen, it is standardly beneficial. That is a key reason why gun advocates think permitting unfettered private ownership of guns is so important.

PROTECTING OTHERS FROM AGGRESSION

It is not simply that guns are often the best means of protecting oneself, they are sometimes the best means of protecting *others*, especially if people are (generally) legally permitted to carry firearms outside the home. After the massacre of elementary school children in Newtown, Connecticut, the NRA proclaimed that the massacre would never have occurred had the principal, some teachers, or some staff been armed (LaPierre, W. 2013). Likewise, NRA advocates said that the killings in the Aurora, Colorado, theater, or the killings and wounding of a congressman and a judge in Tucson, Arizona, would not have occurred had some citizens in the theater or mall been armed. These claims might be true. An armed person in the close vicinity of a potential massacre could potentially stop, disable, or kill a spree/rampage killer. Gun magazines regularly carry stories about how one of their readers saved themselves or their children, stopped a robbery, or protected an innocent person. I have no doubt that some of these stories are true, at least in broad brush. When they are true, that is a benefit of private gun ownership.

PROTECTION AGAINST POTENTIALLY TYRANNICAL GOVERNMENTS

Sometimes a government is or could become tyrannical, threatening the lives and livelihood of its citizens. An armed citizenry may be a viable defense against such a government. In some cases, it may be the best defense (Wheeler, S. C., III 2001: 21). It would be implausible to think that armed citizens have never triumphed over a totalitarian regime, stopped a looming genocide, or at least limited the harm the regime caused. Arguably, Syrian resistance to Bashar al-Assad and Libyan resistance to Muammar Gaddafi exemplify efforts to violently thwart a totalitarian government. Whether these provide conclusive reasons for wanting an armed citizenry is something we explore in the evaluation section below, and again, in slightly different form, in the following chapter.

ARMCHAIR ARGUMENTS FOR GUN CONTROL

The Core Fact

All armchair arguments for gun control spring from one core claim: permitting the private ownership of guns will cause an unacceptable level of harm. Some harm is inevitable given that the private ownership of guns is an inherently dangerous activity. In the previous chapter, I used the history of firearms to explain the idea. Here, I amplify on that idea with several armchair arguments.

In saying that owning guns is inherently dangerous, I neither claim nor imply that guns move on their own volition. They do not stand up and shoot people. It is simply to acknowledge the incontrovertible fact that some activities: climbing K2, B.A.S.E. jumping, and Formula One driving are inherently dangerous activities, while eating soup, petting one's dog, and reading a short story are not. This does not mean that everyone who climbs K2 dies or is seriously injured, or that no one is ever harmed while petting her dog. What it does mean is that if the latter happens it is freakish, while if the former does, it is not in the least surprising. Experience shows that some activities are much more likely to cause harm than are others. Privately owning guns is akin to the former activities and demonstrably different from the latter ones.

It is not just a matter of probability. We have a compelling explanation of *why* owning guns is inherently dangerous in ways that many actions, including many dangerous ones, are not. Although some people are probably attracted to racing and B.A.S.E jumping because they are potentially life-threatening, people's do not do these to be harmed, to cause harm, or to threaten harm. The same cannot be said of firearms. As I explained in the first chapter, from their inception, developers strove to make firearms lighter, more mobile, safer for the user, more powerful, more accurate, and faster. In short, they sought to make them more lethal: better able to harm, kill, or threaten harm (Buchanan, B. J. 2006; Chase, K. 2003).

This is not true of most other activities, not even other dangerous ones. Those who climb K2 or race at Indianapolis or B.A.S.E. jump may want to feel the fear they would have if they actually faced death. However, designers of climbing, jumping, or driving equipment have diametrically opposed aims from those developing firearms. The former want to make these activities appear more dangerous than they actually are. Racers and climbers and jumpers are thus able to experience fear while knowing that their chance of dying or being seriously harmed is *relatively* slim.

Second, mountain climbers and race car drivers usually risk harming only themselves. It is possible that a B.A.S.E. jumper might fall onto an unsuspecting pedestrian or that a race car might jump the track and go hurling into spectators populating the stands. However, when this happens, it indicates that something misfired: for example, the parachute malfunctioned or the racetrack barricades were insufficiently high or sturdy. In contrast, when a gun is used to defend oneself, to stop an aggressor, to down an enemy soldier, or to wound a store clerk trying to halt a robbery, the firearms function *exactly* as designed.

Were owning firearms not inherently dangerous, they would be rotten military weapons, flawed hunting instruments, and inadequate means of self-defense. They are valuable to militaries and gun advocates *precisely* because owning them is inherently dangerous. Yet gun advocates seem to forget that the same features that enable firearms to serve beneficial ends when stopping an aggressor also make them effective offensive weapons, effective ways to commit suicide, and more likely to accidentally cause serious harm or death. These outcomes are neither freakishly rare nor surprising when many people have firearms at hand. Although someone could rob or kill someone else, commit suicide, or be accidentally harmed by the misuse of a spoon, foam, or a banana, that is exceedingly unlikely.

Since owning firearms is inherently dangerous, the more widely available firearms are, the more probable it is that people will be harmed or killed. Someone who wants to harm another is more likely to try and to succeed if she has a gun available (Kleck, G. 1997/2006: 217, 229). This does not exhaust the dangers of private gun ownership. Consider two basic facts of human behavior. One, all of us are occasionally exhausted, hurt, envious, or sloppy. Two, people in these states are more likely to do things they would not do when they are calm, rested, happy, and in control. If people in these conditions have lethal weapons, then they are more likely to harm themselves or others.

While the initial armchair arguments placed the burden of proof on advocates of gun control, this core fact about owning guns shifts the burden of proof to the middle of the scale and perhaps in favor of gun control. A main function of government is to protect people from intentional and unintentional harm. People who put lead in paint and asbestos in walls were not trying to harm anyone. However, since these activities do harm people, the government stopped these practices. It saved lives. The same reasoning explains why the government can legitimately consider constraining the private ownership of guns. It seems reasonable to think we may keep some people (five-year olds) from owning any weapons, we may limit which weapons (bazookas or mortars) anyone can own, we may constrain how firearms are acquired (not in yard sales), how they are stored (not on the front porch), or when, if at all, they can be carried (not on airplanes). To decide whether these and other controls are legitimate, we must consider four ways owning firearms arguably increase the risk of harm. Each gives us reason to think that some gun control is permissible. Collectively they suggest that constraining the private ownership of guns will protect people's vital interest in security. Both pro-gun and pro-control advocates think security is important. They just disagree about how best to achieve it.

Four Risks of Harm

INCREASES VIOLENT CRIMES
Firearms are especially effective weapons; criminals often wield them when committing robberies and assaulting others. That is one

reason why having virtually unrestricted private gun ownership is detrimental. Even so, why would this give us any reason to prevent law-abiding citizens from owning firearms? There are three reasons. One, someone may be technically "law-abiding" if she has never been convicted of a crime, yet is a criminal. Two, the fact that someone has been previously law-abiding does not mean she will continue to be. We are reluctant to deny people the right to own a gun since we do not know which people fit this description. However, we can be confident that there are such people. Therefore, we know that by letting currently "law-abiding" people acquire guns, we will let some criminals acquire guns. Three, a number of criminals stole their guns from law-abiding owners (Cook, P. and Ludwig, J. 1996). Criminals who steal weapons may keep them, or they may give or sell them to other criminals. These considerations give us reasons to think about ways we might keep guns out of criminals' hands.

INCREASES HOMICIDES

An assault with a firearm is more likely to end in death. People can be killed by swords, arrows, slingshots, knives, baseball bats, icepicks, and crowbars. However, these are not weapons attackers standardly choose. The first four were once used in ancient war but are not any more unless the soldier is trying to be stealthy. Moreover, I have never heard about a drive-by sword attack or a spree killing with a slingshot. That is not surprising given the nature of these respective "weapons." If one person wants to kill another, especially if the victim is stronger or faster, then the attacker has a compelling reason to use a gun if one is available and to obtain a gun if she does not have one at hand. Moreover, guns make it easier to kill others at a distance. It is easier to grab an available loaded gun and shoot someone rather than to get close enough to thrust a knife into her chest or abdomen. As noted earlier, it is not simply that guns are more easily used to commit planned homicides, they are also more easily used to attack another when one is angry, inebriated, depressed, or in the throes of passion. Whether these costs are counterbalanced by the aforementioned claimed benefits is a question best answered by empirical evidence, which I explore in detail in later chapters.

INCREASES GUN ACCIDENTS

Since having firearms at hand is dangerous in ways that having most other objects at hand—including most weapons—are not, then we should expect that there are more accidental gun injuries and deaths than there are accidental baseball bat deaths or accidental knife deaths. If someone is cleaning a gun and it is loaded, she may accidentally kill herself. If a child is playing with a gun, she may accidentally kill a friend or family member. Of course, that could happen with a steak knife or a tire iron. However, the latter could happen only in unusual circumstances; someone being killed accidentally with a gun is neither unusual nor surprising.

INCREASES SUICIDES

Many men who wish to commit suicide use guns. It is not difficult to see why: they are lethal weapons. Some people will argue that mature, competent adults should have the right to commit suicide. However, if people do not have such a right, then since gun suicides are more often fatal than attempts using other means, then that is a mark against permitting extensive private ownership of them. Especially considering certain facts about adult suicide.

Evidence suggests that many people who attempt suicide do so with little forethought; many who attempt suicide and fail never try again. These facts suggest that many who attempted suicide did not have an unshakeable desire to die. Consequently, if friends or family thwarted her first attempt, that was often sufficient to save the person's life. Therefore, by limiting people's access to especially lethal means of suicide, we can save some adults' lives, people whose initial attempts are one-off occurrences at odds with their more settled preferences.

More importantly, even if it is morally permissible for a competent adult to commit suicide, more or less everyone will agree that children and incompetent adults lack the rational capacity to choose to die. Evidence shows that many teenage suicides are by firearms. When those are the chosen means, their attempts are more often successful. Guns used in juvenile suicides are almost always owned by a family member or the family member of a friend. Limiting access to guns will thus save a number of juveniles' lives. That is an important consideration that should not be ignored. Whether the number is sufficient to justify serious gun control is an issue I consider later.

ASSESSING THE ARMCHAIR ARGUMENTS

Response to Arguments for Gun Control

Advocates for gun control often note that homicides rates are noticeably higher in counties where many citizens have ready access to guns than in countries where such access is severely limited. This is especially obvious in the United States where homicide rates are dramatically higher than in economically, politically, and socially similar countries like Australia, New Zealand, Canada, and the countries of Western Europe. Opponents to gun control often counter that the explanation for the difference in homicide rates is not the increased access to guns but cultural differences. Many who take this tack suggest that higher homicide rates in the United States stem from our heterogeneity relative to these other countries (Kopel, D. B. 1992: 455, 1282). Others claim that political factors explain the differences. They claim, for example, that some countries, like Japan (which has almost no guns and no murders), are more authoritarian than the United States (Kopel, D. B. 1992). This, not guns, explains the higher homicide rates. Of course, even if this is true, the author has to assume that the degree of their authoritarianism is worse than our higher rates of homicides and gun injuries.

These former responses are not implausible. Armchair reasoning, grounded in historical and sociological knowledge, suggests that when there are deep racial, ethnic, religious, and class divisions, there is often increased intergroup violence. Conversely, if a nation's citizens are racially, ethnically, religiously, and economically similar, we might expect to find less violence. Similar evidence suggests that citizens in more authoritarian countries *might* have more characteristics in common, and thus, are less likely to harm their fellow citizens. Although the second suggestion (authoritarianism) might explain some differences in homicides, it seems implausible to think it explains most differences between the United States and most Western democracies. So I focus on the first proffered explanation.

How can we determine which of these two competing explanations is most plausible? I think we should identify other ethnically, religiously, and economically diverse countries (i.e., like the United States in these regards) where there are fewer privately owned guns; then compare their homicide rates with those in the United States. If such countries have lower homicide rates, then we have reason to think gun prevalence and not heterogeneity explains the higher rates. If such countries have roughly similar homicide rates, then it may well be cultural heterogeneity that explains the different homicide rates. We should also examine homicide rates in the United States and see if the most homogeneous states have the lowest homicide rates and the most heterogeneous ones have the highest rates. Whether we can find similar countries and states to make these comparisons is something I examine in the chapter on the available empirical evidence.

Finally, a prudent and intellectually honest gun advocate will not deny that law-abiding citizens occasionally use their guns illegally or that gun accidents happen. Such denials are implausible. What they should argue is that the frequencies of accidents and illicit uses are insufficiently high to counter-balance the benefits of permitting gun ownership.

Responses to Arguments against Gun Control

There are general considerations rebutting all arguments against gun control. There are also some responses to very specific pro-gun arguments outlined earlier. I will address specific arguments before exploring the more general ones.

SPECIFIC ARGUMENTS
Defending others from aggression

Advocates claims guns are effectively used to defend third parties from aggression. I am confident that armed citizens sometimes do save others' lives. I also suspect it happens less often than advocates aver. In the end, how often it occurs is an empirical question that I discuss extensively in chapters 5 through 7. However, there are armchair considerations that should make us skeptical. Gun magazines are filled with stories of people who claim to have saved someone else's life. Given the human tendency to exaggerate our accomplishments (Bar-Ilan, J., et al. 2009), I suspect a few stories are complete fabrications, some consciously omit relevant details, and many are sincere but inaccurate recountings of events (see Sacks, O. 2013: for a story of the author's false, but vivid, memories). Many men brag about their sexual prowess. I suspect some gun owners brag about their firearm prowess. Other times they construe real events in ways that make them a hero. I revisit this possibility in chapter 7 when I more closely examine one story and explore some finer details of a survey by gun-advocate Gary Kleck (Kleck, G. 1997/2006).

Here is one overarching reason to be wary. Consider the multitude of factors that must converge before an armed citizen could stop a pending or ongoing attack. She must be at the right place, at the right time, with no obstacle or person between her and the aggressor. She must see the attacker before the attacker sees her. She must be sufficiently trained (or strikingly lucky) to be able to hit the attacker who is often moving and might be wearing body armor. Moreover, she must do all this in a stressful environment, sometimes with less than ideal lighting (think the Orlando night club). Finally, the person must have the courage to put her own life on the line. All these factors must not only converge, they must also be motivationally potent before the citizen can successfully intervene. However, I suspect these circumstantial stars align less often than advocates suppose. Sometimes a noble attempt may cause more harm. This almost occurred in the tense seconds following the shooting of a congresswoman at a Tucson mall. An armed citizen admitted that he came within a hair of shooting the person who had wrestled the gun from the attacker thinking that he was the shooter (Hennessy-Fiske, M. and Banerjee, N. 2011). Had the man not paused, he could have killed or injured the hero or other bystanders.

In short, although people can and do sometimes save third parties, the real issue is whether it is likely to happen often enough to counterbalance deleterious consequences that arise from having more, and often not well-trained, armed people thrust into stressful and ambiguous situations. Consequently, despite the occasional genuine benefits of having an armed citizen, we cannot straightforwardly infer that it is generally beneficial to arm a significant number of citizens.

We might think that some of these problems would be avoided if the armed citizens were adequately trained. I am confident that this would make a difference. But it would not always help. For instance, although court bailiffs are usually better trained than the average citizen, we know of one case where an offender took a bailiff's gun and killed two people (CNN 2016). I also suspect the NRA and most gun advocates would resist any government requirement that gun owners be (even minimally) trained.

The armchair arguments summarize obvious facts: having many people carrying guns can sometimes prevent harm and sometimes they can cause it. What our armchair arguments do not tell us is which possibility is more common. As the discussion in chapter 5 will show, it is not easy to find empirical evidence that discerns the relative probabilities of each alternative.

Resisting tyrannical governments

Other advocates claim that an armed citizenry is the best protection against tyrannical governments. Although plausible in some cases, there are four reasons to think this is sufficiently rare and is not a compelling reason to permit, let alone encourage, widespread private ownership of guns. (1) It is unclear if the benefits of having an armed citizenry to resist tyrannical governments outweigh the dangers arising from having widespread private ownership of guns, especially since this resistance would more likely be effective only if a majority of citizens were armed. (2) We have no good reason to think that in countries like the United States, where this debate is especially contentious, that the government is likely to become tyrannical. (3) An armed citizenry may bring down a decent, wholly legitimate government as often as—and arguably more often than—it brings down a tyrannical one. This is undoubtedly the most likely scenario in the United States. After all, it was members of the homegrown right-wing militia whose members blew up the federal building in Oklahoma City and took over the Oregon Wildlife Refuge. (4) Even in countries with tyrannical governments, an armed citizenry may be ineffective or even counterproductive against the state's better armed and better trained military. Armed insurrection could easily make a government more repressive.

We can answer (1) only after evaluating the empirical evidence about the costs and benefits of private gun ownership. Number (2) is a serious problem, particularly when paired with (3). Although (4) is certainly not always true, it is difficult to believe that it is never true. I explore these options in more detail in the following chapters.

RESPONSES TO GENERAL ARGUMENTS AGAINST GUN CONTROL

I have argued that owning guns is inherently dangerous. However, even if that gives us *a* reason to think serious gun control is legitimate, it is not a sufficient reason for such control until we (1) determine the strength of many people's desires to own a gun, (2) assess the difficulty of enforcing restrictions on the private ownership of guns, and (3) evaluate the empirical evidence of the costs and benefits of the private ownership of guns. So an overall assessment of the arguments must await the evaluation of (1) and (2) in the final chapter, and an evaluation of (3) in the discussion and evaluation of the empirical evidence.

In the meantime, I identify two potent armchair dilemmas for pro-gun advocates, dilemmas that tilt the overall argument even more in favor of serious gun control.

The first arises from a common argument made by opponents of anything more than the skimpiest of gun control measures: no significant problems can arise from permitting law-abiding citizens to possess guns. Problems arise only when criminals (and, worse still, only criminals) have guns. Gun control limits which guns law-abiding citizens can own, and how they store or carry them; those controls won't restrain criminals' gun behavior. There is a sense in which this claim is true, just not in any way that gives us guidance when deciding who (if anyone) should be permitted to own a gun. Why? The only sense in which the claim is true, it is true by definition. Let me explain. "Law-abiding" could mean either that (a) the person has not yet broken the law, *nor will they ever do so*, or it could mean simply that (b) the person has not, *until now*, broken the law. If those offering this argument use the first sense of "law-abiding," then their claim is true but trivially so: it is true by definition. No evidence *could possibly* falsify it. For once the formerly law-abiding person used a gun criminally, then she would no longer be law-abiding. However, this trivially true interpretation gives us no guidance whatsoever when deciding whether to give Joan or Jim or Jill a permit to own a gun.

Or the claim might simply mean that (b) the person has not, to date, violated the law. Knowing her previous behavior *might* give us *some* reason to think that she will not violate the law in the future. Some reason, but far from conclusive. We know that if we permit all previously law-abiding citizens to own guns, we know full well that some of them will eventually commit a crime. Some such people kill spouses, perhaps in a jealous rage; nearly half of all women killed are killed by a romantic partner (Khazan, O. 2017). Some people will kill strangers after a fender-bender; some people will kill another following a minor altercation in a local bar or movie theater (Almasy, S. 2014).

As I noted earlier, these are predictable consequences of having widely accessible firearms. When one or more disputants have easy access to a gun, a minor altercation may morph into murderous rage.

Finally, if it were true that previously law-abiding citizens were less likely to use guns to harm others—a plausible claim, I would think— then that would give us a reason to find a method of assuring that only currently law-abiding citizens would have private access to guns. This is precisely why gun control advocates propose, among other measures, thorough background checks before the state permits someone to purchase a gun. The purpose of these checks is to ensure that the purchaser is neither a criminal nor mentally ill. However, many pro-gun groups are opposed to detailed background checks. They certainly oppose requiring registration of guns obtained as a gift or through a private transaction. This gives shape to a significant dilemma for gun advocates. If these advocates really believe it is bad for the "wrong" people to have access to guns, then they should support controls that make it less likely that such people obtain guns. If so, then they should support requiring background checks for those who wish to purchase a gun. Since many do not support these measures, it appears they are not really committed to keeping guns out of the "wrong" people's hands. They cannot have it both ways.

A gun advocate could claim that although my reasoning is right as far as it goes, I ignore other reasons for rejecting background checks. There seems to be only one objection that might do the trick, namely, that there are counterbalancing negative consequences of requiring such checks. Advocates might claim, for instance, that a robust registration scheme would make it too easy for a wayward government to confiscate all citizens' guns. For reasons I mentioned earlier, this is not a serious fear in places like the United States. What is more relevant at the moment is that if that is their real objection, then the initial objection to gun control (depriving law-abiding citizens of the ability to own a gun) was a diversion or at least mis-described. What is doing the work here is not an amorphous belief that law-abiding gun owners do not cause harm with their guns, but rather a conviction that one particular form of gun control—background checks— is unacceptable. If this is their argument, then it is incumbent on them to explain why and how such a seemingly innocuous practice could have such detrimental consequences. After all, we take registration for granted for many other activities (driving a car, prescribing medications, building houses, etc.). We do not get apoplectic at the mere suggestion that we require such registration. Finally, they should propose others means of achieving the same ends less intrusively. The problem is that it is difficult to imagine how these ends could be achieved without background checks or something functionally equivalent to them.

Gun rights' advocates face a second and seemingly more devastating dilemma. This dilemma arises from their response to common armchair arguments for serious gun control: a number of gun deaths occur accidentally, impulsively, or because children use easily accessible guns to kill themselves or someone else. Gun advocates acknowledge that all these happen. However, they claim they happen only because gun owners (a) leave their guns loaded (b) where they might discharge accidentally, (c) where children can get them, and (d) where angry or jealous or rash people have quick access to them. These deaths would be far less common if guns and ammunition were stored correctly.

There's the rub. I agree that *if* private gun owners kept their guns unloaded and secured in safes, then the number of gun accidents, child homicides, and spur-of-the-moment homicides would drop precipitously. However, most gun advocates eschew these practices since it would make it more difficult for them to access a gun if they need to defend themselves from attack or robbery, either in the home or in public.

Gun advocates want two incompatible ends: they want to keep guns at hand so they can effectively defend themselves quickly, *and* they want them kept them in places and ways that make gun accidents, child homicides, and unpremeditated murders less likely. They cannot have both. Either guns will be less accessible for self-defense, or they will be more accessible to children, jealous spouses and lovers, and short-tempered acquaintances or family members.

SUMMARY OF ARMCHAIR ARGUMENTS

The balance of armchair arguments favors moderate to serious gun control. This, though, does not solve the issue. There are three major issues we must still address:

1. We must show that there is not a fundamental or potent derivative moral right to own a gun, certainly not one sufficiently weighty to trump the seemingly good reasons in favor of gun control. I address that issue in the next two chapters.

2. We must show that it is practically feasible to have moderate to serious gun control; that the costs of enforcing such laws are not so high to make the practice infeasible, even if morally warranted. This I address later, especially in the final chapter.

3. We must assess the empirical evidence both for and against gun control and show that the empirical evidence is sufficiently in line with armchair arguments in favor of gun control. The problem, of course, is that there is no scientifically reliable and morally acceptable way of creating and executing studies that meet the highest standards for empirical studies. So we must settle for something less. In chapter 5 I explain this difficulty and offer some suggestions about how we might partly overcome it. In the following two chapters, I outline and assess the empirical evidence at hand.

Chapter 3

A Framework for Rights

Advocates for a serious right to bear arms often employ armchair arguments like some discussed in the previous chapter. They assert that this right is especially valuable; most commonly they claim private gun ownership is a vital means of self-protection. We saw other armchair arguments proclaiming the benefits of private gun ownership; the principal benefit is the use of firearms for protection. In short, the content of rights' claims and the content of claims about the benefits of gun ownership are similar. Despite their similarities, these moral assertions perform different roles on different moral playing fields. Claims about the benefits of private gun ownership are claims expressly about its consequences. Assertions of a serious right to bear arms are standardly offered as contentions about what the government should do without having to engage evidence about the consequences of private gun ownership.

Before I can evaluate the most common popular and philosophical accounts of the right to bear arms in chapter 5, I provide a framework of rights. I identify and discuss two key features of rights; these isolate the function of rights talk in moral and political discourse. Then, I summarize and briefly explore two important distinctions about the nature and character of rights. Finally, I provide a brief snapshot of major developments in human rights thinking. With this information in hand, we can locate gun rights claims on this conceptual matrix. This tripartite discussion sets the stage for the development in the following chapter of the most common arguments for a serious right to bear arms. Using tools presented here, I then evaluate these arguments.

Before I begin, I must emphasize that the gun control debate is moral not legal.

MORAL, NOT LEGAL RIGHTS

In the United States, many pro-gun advocates base their claim of right on the Second Amendment to the US Constitution which reads "A well-regulated militia being necessary to the security of a free state, the right of the people to keep and bear arms shall not be infringed." The reader will quickly notice the introductory clause and might wonder how, if at all, that clause changes the character of the right asserted in the amendment's main clause. People advocating serious gun control could reasonably contend that this clause makes the Second Amendment significantly different from other constitutional rights, for example, those against self-incrimination and for free religious expression. The Second Amendment, they could claim, concerns only members of the official militia, and thus, should not be construed as making any declaration about rights of the average citizen to own guns. Consider the following comparison. Suppose, rather than simply asserting freedom of the press, the First Amendment had said: "An engaged press, being necessary to the furtherance of a free state, the freedom of the press shall not be infringed." Does the qualifying clause change the nature of the press's right? It certainly seems so. This qualification appears to narrow the scope of freedom of the press. It seems plausible to think that a right, so worded, would imply that the work of the press *that promotes informed discussion about important issues and policies*—and thus, enables us to have a genuinely free state—shall not be infringed. Media presentations that do *not* contribute to informed political discussion (e.g., salacious gossip or raw pornography) would not be protected by a right so framed.

I think the introductory clause to the Second Amendment shapes its meaning similarly. If it did not, why include the phrase? Were the authors of the amendments that sloppy with their language? It is implausible to think so.

Although this proposed interpretation of the amendment is highly plausible, the legal argument is currently settled in favor of a general right of citizens to bear arms. In 1998, the US Supreme Court's 5–4 decision in *District of Columbia v. Heller* (554 U.S. 570) held that individuals *qua individuals* have a right to bear arms for self-protection. Citizens do not need to be members of an official militia. Since by law and convention, the meaning of the Constitution is set by the most recent relevant Supreme Court decision, then US citizens do have a *legal* right to bear arms. End of story.

However, the Court's ruling expressly stated that their finding was compatible with numerous forms of gun control. "The Court's opinion should not be taken to cast doubt on longstanding prohibitions on the possession of firearms by felons and the mentally ill, or laws forbidding the carrying of firearms in sensitive places such as schools and government buildings, or laws imposing conditions and qualifications on the commercial sale of arms" (624). So the law, even given this generous (and, I think, misguided) interpretation of the Second Amendment, does not construe gun rights as unusually stringent. In this respect, the Court reflects the claim I advanced in chapter 1: the only options are not simply supporting or opposing gun control. The most plausible policy options are sets of three points, one on each of the three continua: *who* can own *which* gun *in what ways*. The Court's decision was not at—or even near—the extreme of any continuum, let alone all of them.

Although these debates are legally fascinating, they are irrelevant to the current inquiry. We are discussing a moral issue, and moral issues cannot be settled by looking at current law. That is not to say that there is no relation between law and morality. We use moral reasoning to critique, alter, or sustain current law. The law, however, does not resolve moral issues. The Constitution might univocally assert an unfettered right to bear arms, but if citizens should not have such a right, then the law grants the right inappropriately: After all, the original Constitution included provisions that we now deem grossly immoral. For more than eighty years it permitted slavery. For nearly 150 years it forbade women from voting.

The reverse also happens. Perhaps my reading of the Constitution is correct, and individuals who are not part of an organized, legally sanctioned militia should not have a legal right to privately owned firearms. Nonetheless, it might be that morally they should be given such a right. When we consider these possibilities, we see that although constitutional adjudications may be illuminating, they do not straightway settle moral issues.

Finally, US law is decidedly at odds with the legal and moral sentiments in the rest of the developed world. Countries in Western Europe, as well as Canada, New Zealand, and Australia, have far more serious restrictions on firearms than any restrictions within any US state. Doubtless those who support a right to bear arms think these other countries' laws are morally inappropriate. Perhaps they are. My point is simply that the moral issues are primary; consulting current law is never *sufficient* to resolve a moral issue. If it were, those proclaiming a right to bear arms have a justificatory mountain to cross.

This book addresses moral issues, albeit ones with a legal edge to them. Morality concerns not simply what we as individuals should do. The issue of whether one should morally own guns is captured by the fifth continuum described in chapter 1. This book mainly concerns what the law should permit. That is also a moral issue. Among other things, morality concerns the kind of policies and laws we should establish (Feinberg, J. 1984, 1985, 1986, 1988). For the current debate, these issues are captured along the first three (policy) continua: *who* should be able to have *which* guns, and *how* should those people and their guns be regulated.

Before we can answer these questions by an appeal to rights, we need to understand two key features of (almost all views of) rights.

KEY FEATURES OF RIGHTS

Rights as (Side) Constraints

As I mentioned, rights are thought to carry moral weight somewhat independently of the consequences of one's actions. This is true even on views that justify rights consequentialistically, that is, because we judge that a system with rights has better overall consequences than one without them (Sumner, L. W. 1987). Once we determine that you have a right—say, that I tell you the truth—then I should tell you the truth, even if lying in some case has better consequences (Dworkin, R. M. 1977; Scheffler, S. 1992). Some people thus describe a right as a (side) constraint. This idea, made popular by Robert Nozick (2013/ 1974: 29–30), construes rights as *especially* strict limits on when and how people can act to promote the good. Even when theorists do not use Nozick's language, they often accept the broad idea of rights as restrictions on other's behavior, even if they reject his view about the stringency of rights. Raz, for instances, describes rights as "exclusionary reasons" (Raz, J. 1986: chap. 7).

There are contentious debates about what limits a right. Despite these disagreements among major rights theorists, Nozick stands virtually alone in claiming that rights are *almost* inviolable. Most believe that we should sometimes adopt policies that override some citizens' purported rights if the costs of granting the right are substantial. As I noted, the Supreme Court supports myriad restrictions on the right to own a gun: they think we can limit who has guns, which guns they can have, and where they can carry them. Similarly, most theorists (and the Court) think that the rights to free speech, free press, freedom of association, freedom of religious expression, and so forth are also legitimately restricted in some circumstances.

Individuals Have Rights

Some people argue that some groups, and not just the individuals making up the groups, have rights (Appiah, K. A. 2011; Kymlicka, W. 2001). These claims are most commonly made when discussing the historical mistreatment of some groups (African Americans, women, Muslims, etc.) or, relatedly, when advocating multiculturalism. However, even if there are group rights, rights are most commonly thought to be individualistic. That is certainly the focus of the debate over a serious right to bear arms. The problem is that it is not entirely clear what this means. There is one sense in which the claim is indisputably true. You and I and Josephine the Plumber all (individually) have a right to vote. However, that is not to say that the right to vote is unique to any of us. We each have the right because we are people of the appropriate status or have the relevant features (Rainbolt, G. W. 2006: 196–99). In most democracies, non-felon, non-mentally ill citizens over the age of eighteen have a right to vote. Each person has that right because she has the requisite status or features. However, saying that does not make the right collective. It simply reflects the common idea that right tokens (your right to vote) derive from a right type (the right to vote). Rights, no matter how they are justified, are for people (or creatures) *with the required status*, for instance, that they are autonomous or sentient or of a certain age or citizens of a particular town, state, or country. What rights are not is sui generis.

WHAT KIND OF RIGHTS?

For the moment, I set aside the question of who exactly has a right to bear arms. Most people—including the philosophical pro-gun advocates I discuss in chapter 4—acknowledge that there are some classes of people who, at least in principle, should not be permitted to own guns: five-year-old children, current felons, former felons (or at least former *violent gun* felons), people who are seriously mentally ill, perhaps non-citizens (say, illegal immigrants), and probably individuals on terrorist watch lists. Assuming there is a right to bear arms, we ultimately want to ascertain who has it. I suspect doing so will help illuminate both the nature of rights and how they are justified. For instance, if we grant rights to all and only autonomous creatures or all and only sentient creatures, then we can better understand what those rights protect and why they are thought to be valuable. However, I ignore this issue for now and focus on a different question: For those creatures that *do* have the right, what is the right's nature?

Fundamental Rights

In the public debate, almost all pro-gun advocates think there is a serious right to bear arms; many think that the right is fundamental. Unfortunately, I suspect many who make this claim lack a clear sense of exactly what it means. That is not surprising since, as we see later, many contemporary rights theorists have abandoned, or at least downplayed, reference to them. However, we shall assume that there are fundamental rights since many pro-gun advocates believe gun rights are fundamental.

If they are correct, what does that mean? I assume that those who deploy this term think that the right is basic is some way, perhaps akin to other rights explicitly granted in the Constitution: freedom of speech and of the press, freedom of association, freedom of religious expression, and the right to be treated equally under the law. Or perhaps they think they are like rights proclaimed in the Declaration of Independence: life, liberty, and the pursuit of happiness. The view of fundamental treats them as basic. Most people who assert a fundamental right also believe or talk as if they were morally more important than other rights.

However these rights are delineated; if the notion of "fundamental" is to have the moral heft many people attribute to them, we cannot have massive numbers of them. There must be a reasonably small number of them, and the interests they protect should be especially important. If there were hundreds of fundamental rights, the notion would be morally flimsy. There would be no rhetorical or moral benefit of asserting that a particular right is fundamental.

As I mentioned earlier, all rights are (side) constraints. We cannot automatically violate a fundamental right simply because doing so demonstrably benefits most people. A right to free speech cannot be ignored simply because others find my utterances offensive. A right to free religious expression cannot be overridden simply because others find my religion uninformed, silly, or even repugnant.

Derivative rights also constrain appeals to promote the good. These rights are justified by some relationship to fundamental or basic or core rights (Raz, J. 1986: 168). However, since there are additional argumentative steps required to demonstrate the derivation, we may be less confident in the existence of some of these. Perhaps that explains why some people do not think they are as stringent as the right(s) that justified them. I say "normally" since I do not want to foreclose the option, promoted by gun advocates, that the right to bear arms may be quite stringent even if it is derivative.

What makes a right fundamental? There is no account that everyone embraces. Indeed, many theorists no longer employ the language of "fundamental rights." For instance, Martin's authoritative summary on rights makes only passing mention of fundamental rights (2013). Buchanan, in his recent *The Heart of Rights,* uses the phrase once, and then only when discussing someone else's view (2013: 268). However, if there are such rights, what distinguishes them from other rights? I think Shue's description of "basic rights" captures the most plausible meaning of the phrase; I think that is so even if one disagrees with his account of which basic rights we have.

A fundamental right is one that protects some interest "essential to a normal human life" (Shue, H. 1996/1980: 14, 28). If the interests they protect are essential to (any) normal human life, then those interests cannot be unique to any person. The right protects important interests everyone has regardless of any special interests she has or will feasibly develop.

We can distinguish two broad categories of fundamental rights: biological and social. The former protect basic interests required for physical life: food, shelter, and health. Without food and shelter, a person will die. Without a modicum of health, a person will die, or if she lives, she will be miserable and severely disadvantaged. All people have these biological needs no matter what other interests or needs they have.

The latter protect basic interests of civic, social, and personal life. Rights to free speech, association, and religious expression create and sustain a vibrant culture and effective political community; they also empower individuals to make informed, rational choices (Brighouse, H. 2006). We need political and cultural environments in which we can read, think, and speak as we wish, when we wish, and how we wish. Societies without exposure to a diversity of ideas are less likely to be well-functioning. Individuals without exposure to different ideas lack the knowledge they need to have a modicum of control over their lives (Mill, J. S. 1985/1885: chap. 1). We have these important interests no matter what other needs or interests we have.

With this framework in place, we can specify that anyone who claims people have a fundamental right to x should show how and why x is an important interest each person has independently of her unique interests. It is not enough to baldly assert she has a fundamental right to x. Nor does it suffice to assert she knows intuitively which rights she has.

Derivative (Non-Fundamental) Rights

Derivative rights arise from and are justified by fundamental rights. Among other things, that means the reasons for overriding or outweighing a derivative right would generally not need to be as weighty as reasons for overriding or outweighing a fundamental right. This consideration leads various rights advocates to explain why the right, though non-fundamental, is, nonetheless, extraordinarily stringent (Hunt, L. H. 2016: 2444, 2458; Huemer, M. 2003: 299; Hall, T. 2006: 296; Wheeler, S. C., III 2001: 21). There would be no need to make this argument if derivative rights were generally as stringent as fundamental ones.

There are three ways in which a right might derive from a fundamental right, although it is difficult to draw sharp lines between these forms. Few or no pro-gun philosophers have expressly mentioned the first. They focus on the second and third alternatives. I will do the same. Nonetheless, it is worth mentioning the first since someone could develop a theory along these lines.

One, a right might be derivative if it is *implicit* in some number of fundamental rights. The idea is that having all (or some subset) of common fundamental rights would presuppose the existence of another right—for pro-gun advocates, a serious right to bear arms. This strategy might be modeled on the US Supreme Court's reasoning in

Griswold v. Connecticut (381 U.S. 479). In *Griswold,* Justice Douglas said, "In other words, the First Amendment has a penumbra where privacy is protected from governmental intrusion." The idea is this: the five fundamental rights expressly protected by the First Amendment made sense only if individuals had a general right to privacy. The other rights establish a zone within which each individual can act (think, read, associate, pray, etc.) without interference. Although this might be a plausible strategy for defending the right to bear arms, I do not know any gun advocate who has made such an argument, although there are ways of reading Wheeler (1997, 1999, 2001) as flirting with this possibility. Moreover, I am unsure precisely how such an argument would materially differ from the arguments they do make and that I discuss in the next chapter. So I shall not mention this possibility again.

The second form treats the derivative gun right as a *precondition* of a fundamental right. This claim could take a logical, a criterial, or a causal form. A logical precondition identifies certain factors that would have to be true for one to even have the possibility of having (or meaningfully having) some right. Thus, one could not have a meaningful right to free speech if she lacks the ability to communicate with others (e.g., if she were "locked in"). A *criterial* precondition would specify when and how some right was properly ascribed. Thus, one would not have a right to sign legally binding contracts if she were mentally ill, and she would lack a right to vote if she were a seven year old. A *causal* precondition would specify some causal factor(s) that must be present before she is able to have (or at least meaningfully exercise) some particular right. Arguably a person without the ability to travel to a distant voting site or who could not obtain documents required to demonstrate her eligibility to vote would lack an effective right to vote.

As I mentioned, I do not see how the purely logical form could play any role in the gun control debate. However, the other two forms could—and do. Were fundamental rights based on the US Constitution, then the right to bear arms would have a criterial precondition: only an adult US citizen would have this right. The right the bear arms might also be thought to be a causal precondition of other rights. I think this is what Wheeler has in mind when he claims that "gun-ownership rights are a [pre]condition of the practical existence of other rights" (1999: 111). He believes that one cannot confidently exercise any other right if she is incapable of defending herself from an aggressive attack.

The third and most common route is to argue that the right to bear arms is a means to achieve or promote some valuable human interest protected by a fundamental right (Wenar, L. 2011). In a society without a robust safety net, money is a crucial means of satisfying fundamental interests in food, shelter, and healthcare. Pro-gun advocates claim that firearms are a vital means for protecting people's fundamental interest in self-defense. How, though, should we characterize these means? Are they necessary means such that without them the fundamental right cannot be protected? Are they sufficient means such that having them guarantees the protection of the right? Or are they neither necessary nor sufficient? As we shall see, pro-gun advocates disagree about the best way to portray the instrumental role of the right to bear arms. I identify differences between their competing views when I describe the most prominent views in chapter 5.

Positive versus Negative Rights

Many rights theorists distinguish positive from negative rights. There is no wholly uncontroversial way of drawing the distinction (Holmes, S. and Sunstein, C. R. 2000; Lippke, R. L. 1995; Gewirth, A. 2001; Childress, J. F. 1980; Kis, J. 2013). There are cases that do not neatly fit this distinction, no matter how it is drawn (Rainbolt, G. 2014).

For purposes of the current discussion, I offer a common description, one that, among other things, is compatible with the arguments of several key gun advocates.

Here's the idea. Negative rights are rights to the noninterference of others. These rights do not specify what anyone else must or should do; rather they specify only what others should *not* do. Melinda's negative right to life simply specifies that others should not threaten or kill her. Melanie's negative right to free speech simply bars others from stopping her from expressing her views. In contrast, a positive right requires that others sometimes act to enable Melinda (or Melanie or Martha) to satisfy her right. (Shue, H. 1996/1980). If she needs food or healthcare, others should provide them or at least ensure that she can actually obtain them.

Some thinkers deny that there are any positive moral rights. Still others acknowledge that there are such rights; they just believe that negative rights are more stringent—usually much more stringent—than positive ones.

Obviously this is an important distinction when discussing rights to food, education, healthcare, assistance after a natural disaster, and so forth. Does my right to food mean simply that no one can take away food that I have acquired? Or does it mean that I must have the abstract opportunity to obtain the food I need? Or does it mean that I must have the concrete ability to obtain food? Or must it mean that others must help me obtain food if I cannot obtain it myself (e.g., if I am disabled)?

Even if one acknowledges the reality and importance of this distinction when discussing the aforementioned claimed rights, it may not be obvious why and how it is relevant to the debate about a right to bear arms. Here's the explanation. Even if we agree that Sara has a right to own a gun, we must decide what precisely that means. Does that simply mean that others cannot forbid her from owning a gun? Suppose the government does not forbid gun ownership but places a 10% surtax on guns. Sara cannot afford to pay the tax. Does *that* interfere with her right to own a gun? Or suppose Smith and Wesson—along with their competitors—increases the price of guns by 10%. That likewise makes it impossible for Sara (and those like her) to purchase a gun. If the tax is a limitation on their rights, why not the price increase? Or suppose Sara is just poor and cannot afford a gun. Does *that* limit her right? If either of the last two cases *are* limitations on the right to bear arms, then this starts to smell like a positive right to own a gun: for the right to be realized, each person must have the concrete ability to obtain a firearm. It would not be enough to be able to own a gun *if she could afford it*. Determining whether the right to bear arms is positive or negative is relevant to the gun control debate, especially, as we shall see, given some gun advocates' arguments for a derivative right to bear arms.

THE DEVELOPMENT OF RIGHTS TALK

As we will see in the next chapter, pro-gun advocates do not all agree how best to characterize and justify the right to bear arms. The problem is not unique to pro-gun advocates. Rights claims are often asserted excessively, indiscriminately, and imprecisely. Most contemporary major theorists acknowledge that rights theory is in considerable disarray. Each, in his own way, seeks to surmount these problems (esp. Shue, H. 1996/1980; Nickel, J. W. 2007; Griffin, J. 2008; Beitz, C. R. 2009; Buchanan, A. 2013).

To explain how we arrived at this juncture, I briefly survey key moments in the development of rights theories. This is far from a comprehensive account. However, I want to say enough to isolate views of rights most congenial to claims of a serious right to bear arms.

The oldest versions were natural rights theories that grounded rights in divine law. To know which rights we have, we grasp God's commands (St. Thomas Aquinas). Perhaps a variation on this view informed Jefferson's thinking as he proclaimed in the Declaration of Independence, "We hold these truths to be self-evident, that all men are created equal, that they are endowed by their Creator with certain unalienable Rights, that among these are Life, Liberty and the pursuit of Happiness."

By the 1700s, the idea that we needed a deity to explain truth and morality began to lose its grip on many scholars. Even so, many were still drawn to the idea of natural rights. So they searched for ways to maintain the ethics while abandoning the metaphysics. They talked as if rights originated not in the proclamations of a god but arose from human nature. This view motivated John Locke's account of rights (1690) and the Kantian idea that all morality sprang from our nature as autonomous, self-legislating beings (1991/1785).

Although many thinkers since Kant disagree about precisely which rights people have, many adopted the Kantian notion that rights somehow derive from or are connected to human agency. Although Joel Feinberg incorporates elements of Kantian thought, he, like Raz (2010) did not think there was a simple or single way to derive or justify all rights. He thought rights are warranted claims; however, the appropriate way of establishing the warrant may differ. On his and Raz's view, what matters is whether one can defend the claim of right; the arguments for different rights need not have a common foundation. This difference in outlook alters the role of rights claims in specific moral arguments. On their views, claims of rights were conclusions of moral arguments; they were not unsupported premises. Thus, one might say, "I have a right against assault because I can cogently defend the claim that you should not assault me," but not "You ought not to harm me *because* I have a right not to be assaulted." If one's claim that she has a right is standardly the conclusion of a moral argument, then bare rights claims, without any evidentiary edifice, can never resolve a contentious moral debate. Of course, once a claim of right has been established, then the conclusion of the warranting argument *can* be a premise of an argument for a more particular rights claim (Feinberg 1966, 1970, 1980, 1984). However, that rides piggyback on the argument warranting the rights claim.

Feinberg's reasoning sharply contrasts with one of his contemporaries, Robert Nozick. There are two features of Nozick's view of rights that make his account especially attractive to pro-gun advocates: (1) we know which rights we have via intuition, and (2) rights as side constraints are almost inviolable. Intuitionism pervades and informs his arguments. He describes cases about which he thinks all people intuitively know what is right and wrong. He then wields cleverly crafted analogies to extend reasoning to other cases about which we might not be so confident. His persistent reliance on intuitionism is crisply described in Thomas Nagel's forward to the new edition of *Anarchy, State, and Utopia*. "He loved formal structures and logical argument, but his approach to philosophical problems was *fundamentally intuitive*" (2013: 366; emphasis mine).

The second feature is both implicit and explicit in his book (2013/1974: 27-30). Each hypothetical example rests on his conviction that rights can rarely be overridden. He makes this claim expressly in maintaining that rights can be overridden only to avoid "catastrophe" (2013/1974: 180). Whatever "catastrophe" means, it is not just that the consequences are very bad. They must be earth-shatteringly bad. We will see pro-gun advocates' commitment to Nozick's two-pronged approach in several of their arguments for a serious right to bear arms.

Although Nozick's view had significant appeal and considerable staying power in some circles, including among many pro-gun advocates, his contribution to the rights literature was short-lived. Developments since Nozick, especially the seminal works mentioned earlier, reject key features of his views. Nozick is rarely mentioned in the rights literature, and, when he is, his views are quickly dismissed (Griffin, J. 2008: 21–22). These thinkers do not consider his account plausible enough to merit detailed discussion or refutation. However, when reading their accounts, it is clear that a significant element of their disagreement with Nozick is that they reject his suggestion that there is widespread agreement about which rights we have. Griffin contends that we not only disagree about which rights people have, typically there is "no agreement about [even] what is at issue" (2008: 16). The problems with rights talk are so profound that some thinkers contend we should abandon human rights discourse (Glendon, M. A. 1993). Even those who want to keep such talk insist that its reckless use "evoke[s] a disabling skepticism" (2009: 2).

Three of these theorists propose a common solution: meaningful rights talk must be linked to International Human Rights Law (IHRL) as set out in the Universal Declaration of Human Rights (United Nations General Assembly 1948) and in the seventeen subsequent human rights treaties (United Nations 2008).

Beitz contends this approach is more cogent than accounts of rights grounded in privately accessible intuition. "Human rights is a *public* enterprise and those who would interpret its principles must hold themselves accountable to its *public* aims and character" (Beitz, C. R. 2009: iii; emphasis mine). This acknowledgement should inform our thinking about behaviors legitimately controlled by rights:

> Human rights are institutional protections against "standard threats" to urgent interests. A "standard" threat is a threat which is reasonably predictable under the social circumstances in which the right is intended to operate. (2009: 111)

This international turn is also at the center of the latest of these pivotal works. Buchanan spends considerable time chiding philosophers for assuming that there is a meaningful account of rights divorced from IHRL.

> There is no "folk" (that is, widely held, pretheoretical) conception of moral human rights nor any philosophical theory of moral human rights that enjoys this authoritative status. . . . A widespread consensus that individuals' international legal human rights should be realized appears to have developed without being preceded by a widespread consensus on what moral human rights there are. This phenomenon is puzzling, if not inexplicable, if one assumes that international legal human rights are attempts to realize preexisting moral human rights, but perfectly understandable if one rejects that assumption.

With this general view of rights behind us, I can now explain the nature of arguments for a serious right to bear arms. Then I evaluate these claims. That is the task of the next chapter.

Chapter 4

The Right to Bear Arms

DETAILED ARGUMENTS FOR A SERIOUS RIGHT TO BEAR ARMS

I begin this chapter by outlining the most common arguments for a serious right to bear arms. The previous chapter explained why pro-gun advocates want to assert this right. They believe that if there is such a right, it would warrant a serious claim to bear arms without having to significantly worry about either the armchair arguments or the empirical evidence. If gun advocates can deflect the objections posed in the previous chapter, and those that will be offered in three subsequent chapters, then their argument would be morally robust.

Since each pro-gun advocate holds slightly different views and offers slightly different arguments, I will briefly describe and evaluate the most prominent ones. However, I will not become mired in minor squabbles between them; more unites than divides them. All think that (most) citizens have a right to bear (most) arms. All think that right arises *largely* because firearms are a vital means of self-defense. I focus my evaluation on this shared and plausible view. Most who assert such a right claim it is derivative. Two aver that the right is (also) fundamental.

Fundamental Rights

As I explained in the previous chapter, it is rhetorically advantageous to claim that the right to own guns is fundamental. Nonetheless, only two philosophers in the literature explicitly advance this view. Neither spends much time explicating the notion of a fundamental right or explaining why they think a gun right is fundamental. Most of their arguments make it seem as if the right to bear arms is derivative. Indeed, each claims that the derivative right, based on the use of guns for security, is especially stringent. Nonetheless, since they also assert that the right is fundamental, I briefly describe their respective arguments; I evaluate them in the next major section of the chapter.

Huemer's explanation is quite brief. He defines a fundamental right as one that "has some force that is independent of other rights" (Huemer, M. 2003: 299). At the same time, he avers that the derivative right is morally more important (Huemer, M. 2003: 297). I am not confident which of his examples or arguments he believes defend the claim that the right is fundamental. I focus on the one argument that does not expressly treat the right as a means to self-defense. Huemer claims "firearms enthusiasts" have a right to own guns since they enjoy hunting or target shooting. He claims that their "right to entertainment" is morally stringent *and* that the right becomes more stringent as the gun owner's interest in having firearms increases (Huemer, M. 2003: 297–298, 304–305).

> Ceteris paribus, the weight of a fundamental right increases with the importance of the right to an individual's plans for his own life or other purposes. This is not to say that every action that interferes with an individual's aims is a rights violation, but only that if an action violates rights, it does so more seriously as it interferes more with the victim's aims. (2003: 300)

Although many people think recreational activities are insufficiently valuable to ground an important right, he asserts that they hold this view only because they fail to recognize that "recreation is a major source of enjoyment, and enjoyment is (at least) a major part of what gives life value" (2003: 305).

Given the enormous value of these activities, this right morally bars us from interfering with the private ownership of guns even if we knew ownership were to cause others considerable harm. Any harms it caused "would have to be many times greater than the benefits in order for the right to own a gun to be overridden" (2003: 297).

Although Wheeler also claims that the right to bear arms is fundamental, his characterization of and argument for the right, are quite different. He approvingly cites then NRA president Charlton Heston's "suggestion" (Wheeler's words) that gun rights are fundamental since they are a "condition of the practical existence of other rights" (1999: 111). This right is not just *a* precondition, it is *the* precondition to "insure that our rights are respected" (1999: 113). What exactly does this mean? Do I need a gun to engage in free speech or free religious expression? Not ordinarily. So it is not a precondition of any single right. However, if my government is or becomes oppressive, then a right to bear arms becomes a valuable way of protecting all my rights. Thus, I think his claim that a gun right is fundamental is connected to his later and more detailed argument that firearms are a derivative right: they are a vital means for thwarting, undermining, or overthrowing totalitarian regimes. I develop this version later when discussing non-fundamental rights.

Derivative Rights

As I briefly mentioned earlier, a few advocates who claim that gun rights are non-fundamental claim the right derives from a general right to freedom. I briefly address this option in the evaluative section. This form of the argument is less commonly brandished by pro-gun advocates than are ones based on the assertion that guns are vital means of self-defense. I focus on this later form since all pro-gun advocates offer some variation of it, likely because it is the strongest and most plausible.

Most forms of this argument concern self-defense against individual attackers or intruders. Before discussing this more familiar form, I describe a version developed in the philosophical literature by Samuel Wheeler (1997, 1999, 2001). This argument is grounded in self-defense, albeit self-defense against rogue governments.

PROTECTING ONESELF FROM TOTALITARIAN REGIMES
Governments, Wheeler argues, are the primary threats to individual security. It is easy to see why:

> Given that one is a human being who has been subjected to unjust deadly assault since 1900, the conditional probability that the assailants were agents of one's own government is higher than the conditional probability that the assailant is a criminal by local standards of legitimacy. If we leave out cases of questionable injustice, and just include clearly unjust homicides, the totals from the Belgian, Turkish, Russian, German, Chinese, Ugandan, Indonesian, Cambodian, Rwandan, etc., government-sanctioned slaughters exceed the totals from the private sector by a substantial factor. (1999: 114)

History thus shows that we should infer that "it is always reasonable to worry about government injustice, that no institutions will remove the reasonableness of that worry, and that therefore, every just government institutionalizes the possibility of resistance to it" (1999: 115). So even if we didn't have a reason to protect ourselves from potential personal attacks, we have compelling reason to protect ourselves against possible government coercion. He offers two historical examples to illustrate his claim:

> It is obvious that the residents of the Warsaw Ghetto had a right to defend themselves and that each member of a Cambodian village had a right to resist "relocation" by the Khmer Rouge, even though the governments assaulting them were "legitimate" in the sense that they had been recognized by other governments. (1999: 115)

Although private citizens are usually disadvantaged when fighting organized military units, "firearms, even of very disparate power, tend to level the odds in a confrontation.... [T]he danger and uncertainty of coercion [for the state] is increased by several orders of magnitude when there is an armed citizenry" (1999: 119).

Although it might seem prudent to want a society with fewer guns and less violence, that is "unjustified optimism, short-sightedness, and unwarranted smugness" (1999: 122). Things change. Even good governments can become vicious. Hence, it would be prudent for us to resist attempts to *disarm* [emphasis mine] the population (1999: 123). That is one compelling reason why we have a right to bear arms.

SELF-DEFENSE AGAINST PERSONAL ATTACKS

The most common pro-gun argument might be summarized thusly:

a) Everyone has a right of self-defense against individual aggressors.
b) Guns are the only (or best or most reliable or most effective or most reasonable) means of self-defense against aggression, either in or away from one's home.
c) Therefore, people have a right to own—and usually to carry—a gun.

Before exploring their respective views, it is important to notice that Huemer, Wheeler, and Hunt explicitly target the view that we should ban firearms. (Wheeler, S. C., III 1997: 423; 2001: 20; Huemer, M. 2003: 304, 308–11; Hunt, L. H. 2016: 138, 720) Although Hall (2006) does not expressly do the same, it seems that is the policy at which most of his arguments are aimed. This emphasis seems peculiar since none of the most common gun control proposals in the United States are gun bans. Indeed, as I explained in the first chapter, virtually no one holds the extreme on any of the three policy continua, let alone all of them. Virtually no one wants everyone banned from owning any firearm. Some policies ban some people (e.g., mentally ill people and children and former violent gun felons) from owning guns; others ban *some* types of firearms (mortars or assault weapons); still others restrict the ways guns are acquired or transferred; they also specify where owners may not carry guns, for example, on airplanes and in other gun-free zones (schools, government buildings, bars, etc.).

Does that show that the pro-gun philosophers are railing against a view no one holds? Perhaps. However, we should assume that they see themselves as engaged in the current debate. Therefore, I speculate that they embrace something akin to the following unstated assumption: if it is wrong to ban guns, then we can (fairly) straightforwardly infer that many—and probably most—gun control policies are unjustified and unjustifiable. That something akin to this assumption is at work is explicitly stated by Huemer (2003: 304, fn 14) and implied by Hunt (2016: vi). Whether this is a plausible assumption is an issue I address obliquely in the remaining chapters.

What Does "Means" mean?

All pro-gun authors see gun ownership as a means of self-defense. However, they do not agree about the meaning of "means." I think any final account of a derivative right to bear arms should explain precisely what "means" means in this context. However, I want my assessment to be applicable to all gun advocates' views. So I will not shoehorn them into a single mold. Still, it is worth summarizing their diverse accounts of "means." This will inform some later evaluation.

A NECESSARY MEANS

Huemer appears to hold that guns are a necessary means of self-defense. He describes two behaviors he claims we intuitively know are wrong, behaviors he contends are morally analogous to depriving people of a right to bear arms. Since the behaviors are wrong, banning guns would also be wrong. Here are his examples: (1) confiscating a gun that a victim could have used to prevent her death, and (2) holding a victim while someone else stabs her. He contends these analogical arguments show that a gun ban would be an instance of "preventing the prevention of a death. . . . [This] is about as serious a wrong as killing." A ban would override the "self-defense rights of noncriminal gun owners. . . [purportedly] to protect society from criminal gun owners" (2003: 307–308). These examples suggest he thinks that without a gun many people would be unable to defend themselves; he thereby implies guns are a *necessary* means for self-defense, at least for some number of people.

However, he does not think that we must permit *all necessary* means to self-defense. We can imagine situations where the only way of protecting oneself from a horde of crazed killers would be with a mortar, a bazooka, or a howitzer. If people had a right to all necessary means of self-defense, then people would have a right to these weapons. He contends, however, that that would be absurd (2003: 323, fn 56). He does not explain why. I infer that he relies on something like the following plausible argument: there is no way to provide the right to own a mortar in all and only those cases where having one is necessary for self-defense. The only way we can provide the right in these rare cases is by permitting all (or most) adults to own them. That would be too risky. Therefore, there cannot be a right to own mortars (or other heavy weapons). If this is his argument, it suggests that he holds something like the following view: people have a right to only those firearms that are necessary means of self-protection for *a sufficiently large* number of people in a *significantly large* number of circumstances. I see no other rationale for claiming that we should permit people to have the necessary means for self-defense while *categorically* rejecting the claim that people have a right to privately own mortars.

Hall, Hunt, and Wheeler reject Huemer's suggestion that we have a right to bear arms because guns are a *necessary* means of self-defense. They offer alternative accounts.

A REASONABLE MEANS

Hall advances what he dubs the "reasonable means" formulation. He claims firearms are especially effective defensive weapons since they

> are capable of inflicting devastating injuries immediately. Guns are easy to use, and easy to learn to use, even for individuals lacking physical strength, coordination, or experience in hand-to-hand combat. Guns can be effectively employed by a single, physically weak defender even against multiple assailants. Guns can be used far enough from one's target to leave the gun owner safe from counter attack other than, perhaps, by a gun-toting criminal. (2006: 304)

Hall contends these facts show that the grounds for a right to bear arms is not that they are a necessary means of self-defense, but rather that they are sufficient means that should be available at a reasonable cost (2006: 301-303). This does not require that everyone has the *actual* means of such defense. That misconstrues the nature of the right. A gun right is purely negative. It requires only that the state "not act so as to deny all reasonably costly means for the satisfying of an important interest that would otherwise be available" (2006: 302–304). Of course, a cost that most people find reasonable may be beyond some people's financial reach. Even so, on Hall's view, those people would still have a negative right to bear arms.

AN EFFECTIVE MEANS

Hunt denies that citizens have a right to any possible means of self-defense; he does not want them left with no means of exercising their rights of self-defense (2011: 115). So what is a pro-gun theorist to do? The most viable alternative is to construe the means right as a right "against others, that they not coercively prevent one from acquiring or using *some* means of exercising an option-right" (2016: 38; 2011: 116; emphasis mine). If the government stops someone from obtaining a gun or stops her from using it to protect herself, *then* it violates her right of self-defense. However, no "option-right could be so powerful as to transform every means to exercising it into a right." We need "a more moderate view." Hunt proposes the Principle of Effective Means:

> An option-right includes, as an essential component, a right to acquire and use an effective means of exercising it (provided this means is acquired and used without wrongdoing), where "effective means" is understood as one that affords the agent a substantial assurance of achieving the goal that is internal to the act-type that the option-right entitles one to perform or, failing that, comes as close to that level of assurance as can be achieved. (2016: 49-50; 2011: 126)

This principle requires only that the government permit means that are most likely to assure success (also, see Wheeler, S. C., III 1999: 111). In the case of self-defense, "it is on the face of it extremely plausible that the best means in many cases (though not in all) is a handgun" (Hunt 2016: 52; 2011: 127). Nonetheless, the right is not absolute. The right does not give one the authority to violate another's right (2016: 48-49). We must also be certain that allowing people to own guns does not subject others to unacceptable risks. However, he thinks neither qualifier is a problem for gun advocates. One, he contends that the circumstances in which a noncriminal gun owner would violate someone else's rights would be rare while the benefit of owning guns is enormous. Two, he thinks concerns about risks to others is largely misguided. Some risky actions (e.g., using dynamite) simply cannot be performed "in a completely safe manner" (2016: 70). Owning guns, he claims, is nothing like this. "Modern guns are precision instruments.... Following simple rules ... makes it *impossible* to harm someone unintentionally (2016: 71-72; emphasis mine).

EVALUATING THESE CLAIMS OF RIGHTS

Theoretical Objections

Neither the Universal Declaration of Human Rights (United Nations General Assembly 1948) nor any of the seventeen subsequent human rights treaties (United Nations 2008) recognize "a right to bear arms." Only the Arms Trade Treaty of 2013 mentions guns, and the function of that treaty is to discourage the transfer of guns between countries (Final Conference on the Arms Trade Treaty 2013). Of course, the fact that these documents do not acknowledge this right does not *prove* that there is not one. It is, however, compelling reason to reconsider one's confidence in asserting it. One would expect that if there were a moral right to bear arms, it would merit mention in IHRL. This body of law has a long intellectual history; it reflects the thoughts of many moral and legal experts from widely diverse cultures.

Gun advocates' use of rights is likewise at odds with the views expressed and the reasoning employed in seven key philosophical works on human rights written over the past four decades (Shue, H. 1996/1980; Raz, J. 1986: chap. 7; Rainbolt, G. W. 2006; Nickel, J. W. 2007; Griffin, J. 2008; Beitz, C. R. 2009; Buchanan, A. 2013). None of these authors asserts, or seriously discusses, a right to bear arms. This suggests that these theorists think there is no such right, or that if there is, it is insignificant.

It is not simply that these pivotal philosophical theorists do not advocate a right to bear arms, they talk about rights very differently than do gun advocates. Rather than baldy asserting the presence of any right, these theorists vigorously defend rights assertions, while many gun advocates seem to assert rights claims cavalierly. The promiscuous use of rights language leads many theorists to express skepticism about them. As James Griffin puts it:

> The term "human right" is nearly criterionless. There are unusually few criteria for determining when the term is used correctly and when incorrectly—and not just among politicians, but among philosophers, political theorists, and jurisprudents as well. The language of human rights has, in this way, become debased. (2008: 14–15)

Although these thinkers have misgivings with much rights talk, they do not abandon it. Each expends significant intellectual energy trying to salvage some remnants of it. Nickel, Beitz, and Buchanan think that if rights have an intellectual future, it is by yoking them to the content, nature, and function of international human rights law. That requires understanding that people live in modern states. We must then determine what states should not do to, and should do for, their citizens. We must also ascertain when citizens of other states may legitimately intervene if another government is not respecting its citizens' rights. Exactly how a right to bear arms might fit into this approach is something I consider in the next section.

Theoretical options

Despite the above stated problems, gun advocates are not without theoretical resources. I see three ways gun advocates might locate an assertion of a serious right to bear arms within rights thinking. Gun advocates could embrace Nozick's view of rights: rights are known intuitively, they are wholly negative, and they are virtually inviolable. These are all prominent elements of pro-gun thinking. However, as I explained in the previous chapter, Nozick's view has effectively vanished from mainstream discussion of rights. His views do not merit detailed discussion by any of the seven rights theorists I cited earlier. Most never mention him. Those that do quickly dismiss him (Griffin, J. 2008: 21). Among the pro-gun advocates, even Hunt, whose work seems most indebted to Nozick, expressly criticizes him. He claims that Nozick erroneously treats rights as almost inviolable and fails to recognize the existence of positive rights (Hunt, L. H. 2016: 2026, fn 20). Although some gun advocates might seek to resurrect Nozick's take on rights, I explain in an earlier work why I think that enterprise is doomed (LaFollette, H. 1979). Several arguments later in this chapter expose some significant weaknesses of his views.

Second, someone might use Beitz's approach and argue that firearms empower citizens to defend themselves from "standard threats." Whether this move is plausible depends upon empirical evidence about the nature and frequency of threats, as well as information about countervailing costs of allowing relatively unfettered private ownership of guns. I explore the available empirical evidence in the next three chapters.

That said, one advantage of this approach would be that pro-gun advocates could use it to explain why they advocate controlling heavy firearms. They claim people should not be permitted to own bazookas or mortars (Huemer, M. 2003: 323; Hunt, L. H. 2016: 643; Hall, T. 2006: 295). Although someone could face multiple attackers where having a heavy firearm would be advantageous (or even necessary) for self-defense, such situations would be exceedingly rare. Therefore, people do not need these weapons to defend themselves from *standard threats*.

This approach is related to a third option—one I think best reflects the words and spirit of most pro-gun arguments. They could (a) embrace Feinberg's, Shue's, and Rainbolt's view that rights are warranted claims (Feinberg, J. 1966, 1970; Shue, H. 1996/1980: 18–19; Rainbolt, G. W. 2006), and then (b) argue that a serious right to bear arms is warranted. This is a plausible way of constructing their most common argument for a derivative right to bear arms. Although promising, this approach comes at a cost: advocates now carry the argumentative burden of establishing that firearms *are* the best or most reasonable or most effective means of defending oneself—*and* that the costs of gun ownership are not too high. Moreover, by taking this approach they abandon one impetus for asserting a serious right to bear arms: to assert a moral claim to guns without having to rely significantly on the armchair and empirical arguments. They must, instead, carefully examine these arguments, something they seem loath to do. However, before I examine the arguments for a derivative right to bear arms, I briefly explain why the right is not fundamental.

Why They Are not Fundamental Rights

The ordinary person on the street might think that the right to bear arms is fundamental. However, as I noted previously, only Michael Huemer and Samuel Wheeler III expressly forward this claim, and neither puts a premium on it.

Huemer's claim rests on intuition (Huemer, M. 2003: 297). None of the major rights theorists mentioned earlier give intuition a central role in his theory. Rightly so, I think.

One, Sinnott-Armstrong explains why we should not rely on intuition in moral discussions. "The fact that our moral intuitions *seem* justified does not show that they really *are* justified" (2008: 761; emphasis in original). We have compelling evidence that framing effects (the way questions are worded) alter people's intuitive responses to real and imaginary cases. Since we cannot trust those judgments, we are not "justified noninferentially [without accompanying argument] in trusting moral intuitions" (2008: 1047–1048).

Two, although some philosophers give credence to intuitions, few think they are unassailable. Many think we should not accept them in isolation from other moral considerations, especially widely accepted moral principles (McMahan, J. 2013: 111–114).

Three, we have reason to doubt the gun advocates' intuitions since they clash with the best rights theories, with International Human Rights Law, and with the moral beliefs of a sizeable majority of people in the developed world. Of course the majority may be mistaken. However, the burden is on gun advocates to show that they are mistaken. They should not simply assert via intuition that the majority is misguided.

Four, a passing glance at human history reveals numerous instances where people used "moral intuitions" to justify grotesquely immoral actions. People intuitively knew that slavery was not only permissible but perhaps obligatory, and that women should be denied the vote. Growing up I "intuitively knew" that I should not have to eat in the same restaurant, use the same toilet, or live in the same neighborhood with African Americans. I was shamefully wrong. We should be exceedingly cautious when relying on moral intuitions (LaFollette, H. 2017). Too often these are simply cover for ordinary prejudices.

Wheeler defends the claim that the right is fundamental differently. He asserts that the right to own a gun is a "condition of the practical existence of other rights" (1999: 111). The idea, I take it, is that the government may trample on a person's rights if she lacks the wherewithal to violently thwart it. This idea requires explication since it seems improbable to think that having a gun is the only way to resist efforts to suppress one's speech or religious expression. It is not simply that this is not the only means, it is normally not a morally acceptable response to the violation of a single right. As I suggested earlier, the only possible circumstances in which one may need a gun to protect her rights is if her government is not squelching the exercise of this or that right, but if it has become totalitarian and all her rights are in jeopardy. That is why I think this argument rises or falls with Wheeler's derivative argument that we need armed citizens to resist repressive regimes. Claiming that the right to own a gun is fundamental does not carry any argumentative weight here.

The notion of a fundamental right needs more philosophical heft than these gun advocates provide. As I explained in the previous chapter, fundamental rights are standardly understood as ones "essential to a normal human life" (Shue, H. 1996/1980: 14, 28). If pro-gun advocates assert that they have a fundamental right to bear arms, they must show how and why this is a *fundamental interest* each person has *independently of her particular interests*. It is unclear how such an argument could get off the ground. Guns are not "essential to a normal human life." This is not to dispute that, for some people in relatively unusual circumstances, guns may be the most reliable, or even the only, means of self-defense. However, that does not show that owning guns is *generally and usually* vital for an individual's security. The majority of people living in Europe and in the United States do not own guns and they flourish. In contrast, no one could flourish without food, water, and health. No one could be an active citizen in a vibrant and effective democracy without basic civil liberties. These rights protect interests that are not circumstance- or person- specific. That is why some people contend these biological and civil rights are fundamental and why a serious right to bear arms is not.

Gun advocates might try a different tack. They might claim that a right to security is fundamental. Since they think that owning guns is the best way of defending *that* right, then owning guns is a means of protecting a fundamental right (Wheeler, S. C., III 1999: 113; 2001: 21). This construes the right to a gun as a means right; I focus on that claim later.

There is an additional problem worth mention: pro-gun advocates construe security narrowly. They seem to think that my security depends entirely on whether I have a right to a gun. That claim ignores significant elements of security.

> Basic rights are a shield for the defenseless against some of the most devastating and most common of life's threats. . . . [They] are a restraint upon economic and political forces that would otherwise be too strong to be resisted. They are social guarantees against actual and threatened deprivations of at least some basic needs. (Shue, H. 1996/1980: 18)

Various IHRL documents take a similar stance. The threats most people face are not ones that could be protected with a gun. Security is most commonly protected by laws and policies that ensure a person does not starve, is not homeless, and can obtain healthcare. Far more people die from deprivation than die because they did not have a gun at hand. That is not to say that people never face threats to their physical security. However, when they do, there are multiple ways to cope with them. We may hire more police, place locks on our doors, get large dogs, install security systems, or purchase a gun. It *might* be that having a gun is the most effective means for protecting oneself from physical assault. If that is what the empirical evidence shows, then that would be a reason why people should be permitted to obtain guns. However, gun advocates cannot plausibly assert this claim sans evidence.

We should also not forget that many people find the world threatening in part because so many people have guns. Hall should have noticed that the reasons people want guns for self-defense (Hall, T. 2006: 304) are the same reasons criminals want them. With one important difference: criminals are probably more adept at using guns than are most citizens who want them for self-defense. Moreover, some who carry assault weapons openly do so not to defend themselves but to menace others. That seems undeniably true of the armed militia who confronted the Bureau of Land Management workers trying to confiscate Cliven Bundy's cattle. Bundy had refused to pay grazing fees for years; he owed the government more than one million dollars (Domonoske, C. 2017). At the time, federal officials backed down rather than risk a pitched battle. That, of course, was precisely what the armed ranchers wanted. The same motive was doubtless at work when forty heavily armed men appeared outside a Texas restaurant where a group of mothers advocating gun control were meeting (Stanglin, D. 2013).

I suspect these instances help explain why a majority of US citizens feel less safe if they know their neighbors have guns. In a survey of more than 2,500 randomly selected people, only 14% said they would feel safer knowing their neighbors had guns (Miller, M., Azrael, D., and Hemenway, D. 2000: 710). Perhaps more surprising, although gun owners are more likely than non-gun owners to say they feel safer if their neighbors are armed, still, fewer than one-third agree (Miller et al. 2000: 713). Apparently they do not believe the claims standardly made by pro-gun advocates: more guns make people safer (Hunt, L. H. 2016: 72-74; Lott, J. R., Jr. 2010/2000/ 1997). This consideration plays a key role in DeGrazia's argument that people have a right to be secure from the dangers posed by gun owners (DeGrazia, D. 2016: chap. 14). Although I am sympathetic to his argument, I will not discuss it here; those interested should read his discussion. I think the objections I raise here and later are sufficient to undercut the pro-gun advocates' arguments.

Rights to Entertainment

As I noted earlier, Huemer's right to entertainment has some elements that make it look like a fundamental right and others that make it look like a derivative one. So I shall discuss it as a bridge between the previous examination of fundamental rights and the upcoming extended examination of derivative rights.

Huemer is correct that we highly value "nonreproductive sexual activity, reading fiction, watching television or movies, talking with friends, listening to music, eating dessert, going out to eat, playing games, and so on" (2003: 305). I agree. Most everyone would. However, this does not show that gun control is inappropriate. First, since the recreational gun uses Huemer mentions (target shooting and hunting) are legal virtually everywhere, the examples are tangential to gun control proposals that are the focus of this book. Even in countries with *very* serious gun control, one can target shoot at "shooting clubs." Second, the behaviors he claims are analogous to serious gun control are nothing like gun control. The behaviors he describes are permissible precisely because they do not standardly harm anyone. We would evaluate these behaviors differently if they were risky. If we discovered that reading fiction caused bystanders to develop brain cancer, we would almost certainly restrict it. After all, we already evaluate these behaviors differently when they do cause harm. Many states and countries forbid an HIV-positive person from having unprotected (recreational) sex with people who do not know his condition. These considerations show that Huemer's examples relevantly differ from proposed limits on the private ownership of guns. So I set this argument aside and examine the far more plausible derivative right to own guns that springs from people's right to self-defense.

Are Gun Rights Derivative Rights?

There are two distinct but overlapping forms that derivative rights to bear arms take in the literature. One, advocates claim that people have a right to freedom. They then contend that if people want to do X, then they have a prima facie derivative right to do X, although that right may be overridden if X harms others. I assume this is what Hunt wants to capture in claiming that the right to bear arms is an "option right."

The second and most common form is distinct from, but related to, the first. Advocates claim that people have a right to self-defense. Since guns are the only or best or most reasonable or most efficient means of defending oneself, then people have a derivative right to own guns.

Since the second is by far the most common argument used by gun advocates, then that is the form on which I focus. Still, I briefly evaluate the first form since it is sometimes paired with the second.

I am not opposed to saying that a right to bear arms is derivative from a general right to be free. That is, if there are no countervailing reasons, then it is plausible to think that people have a right to own a gun. This is not much of an admission. A right to bear arms would thus be akin to the "right" to eat a Popsicle, walk backward across the living room floor, shop at Home Depot, or cook a Thai meal. We could call these rights. However, little hangs on doing so since, except in bizarre circumstances, we cannot imagine how these actions might harm others, or why everyone, or even some subclass of people, should be prohibited from doing them. We would not legally bar four-year-olds from eating Popsicles, mentally ill people from shopping at Home Depot, or violent felons from cooking Thai food. Circumstances are quite different, however, when it comes to owning guns. There *are* reasons for forbidding four-year-olds, seriously mentally ill people, and former violent felons from owning guns.

What these examples show is that whether we should permit or prohibit some action cannot be settled simply by knowing what people want to do. We disallow many behaviors people might want to do: robbery, embezzling, or driving 60 mph in a school zone. We do not (now) let oil producers add lead to gasoline or contractors to install asbestos-based insulation. We forbid these actions because we have good empirical evidence of the significant costs of doing so. Other behaviors—talking with friends, reading philosophy, and eating asparagus—we permit because we have no reason to think these harm others.

If letting people own guns is beneficial and has few costs, then the claim that people should be allowed to own them is highly plausible. However, we know from the armchair arguments that owning guns is dangerous in ways that owning pencils and telephones is not. That makes the claim of a right to bear arms relevantly different from claims about the trivial derivative rights mentioned earlier. That is why arguments based on the use of guns for self-defense are so critical to this debate. They are gun advocates' best hope.

Self-Defense Arguments

I earlier described two forms of the argument from self-defense. Although I discuss them separately, it should be apparent that they have similar forms and face similar objections. I discuss the less familiar form first and in detail. I isolate a series of questionable unstated assumptions in and difficulties for Wheeler's argument. Then I examine the second and most common form.

This provides us an opportunity to explore the significance of asserting that the serious right to bear arms is a means right. Something can arguably be a means right only if we have evidence (a) it is an effective means to a valuable end and (b) exercising the right does not cause others undue harm. Anecdotes can never establish either claim. That is why the plausibility of *this* rights claim cannot be divorced from the empirical evidence I discuss in chapters 5 through 7. This will become more obvious as I develop objections to these derivative rights.

DEFENDING ONESELF FROM PUTATIVELY
TOTALITARIAN REGIMES

As I explained earlier, Wheeler argues that we need armed citizens to resist totalitarian regimes. Let us grant that governments are sometimes serious threats to citizens' security. Let us also grant, for purposes of argument, that the governments of each regime he identified were totalitarian. Would these facts have justified the citizens' rebelling against them? Not without more information. Responsible rebels should also want good reasons to think (1) there is no viable alternative to violent revolution; (2) there is a reasonable chance they can remove the deplorable regime; (3) they can do so without excessively harming others; and (4) they can replace the despicable regime with a morally superior one.

If these conditions look familiar, there is a reason. They parallel those of standard Just War Theory. The assumption that the government is totalitarian is akin to the just cause criterion. The first condition is effectively the last resort criterion. The second is the reasonable chance of success criterion. The last two are subdivisions of the proportionality criterion. The parallel should not be surprising. The criteria for a just rebellion should arguably parallel those for a just war.

It is not enough that the criteria for armed rebellion *be satisfied* from some god's eye view. Nor it is enough that the rebels *sincerely believe* that they are satisfied. The rebels should *reasonably believe* that they are satisfied. If they do not have evidence that the criteria are satisfied, then the rebels would have no moral reason to act. Neither bare truth nor sincere belief is sufficient to justify individual acts of rebellion, just as they are insufficient to justify going to war.

We can see the importance of these criteria once we examine Wheeler's examples. Armed insurgents brought three of these despicable totalitarian regimes to power. The Bolsheviks violently overthrew tsarist Russia; Mao tossed out Chiang Kai-shek, who himself had consolidated power after overthrowing the last Manchu emperor; Pol Pot ousted Lon Nol's regime, which came to power some years earlier when Nol overthrew Prince Sihanouk. Admittedly, none of the overthrown regimes were model governments. However, it seems that the new regimes were almost certainly worse than the ones they replaced (Snyder, T. 2010).

Wheeler certainly thinks so. He thinks it is obvious that these replacement regimes were serious threats to *their* citizens, and therefore were instances where citizens would have been justified in violent overthrowing them. What he fails to see or acknowledge is that the reasoning that he thinks justified rebellion *against* them would have also justified *their* rebellions against the governments they ousted. In each case, the rebels thought the existing regimes were coercive.

The same reasoning would have also have justified the South's armed rebellion against the North, as well as armed resistance against efforts to end segregation. The bombing of the Birmingham church, the uptick in the lynching of blacks, and the murder of numerous civil rights workers and leaders, and so on would all seem to have been justified if rebellion were permissible as long as citizens *sincerely believed* that their government was engaging in unjust coercion.

These examples should make citizens cautious before assuming that they are justified in using violent means to oust regimes they deem totalitarian, especially given the extensive evidence that most of us lack reliable self-knowledge and have trouble making informed predictions about the likely outcomes of our actions (e.g., a rebellion) (Pronin, E. 2009; Pronin, E. and Kugler, M. B. 2007; Pronin, E., Lin, D. Y. and Ross, L. 2002; Burton, R. A. 2009; Tversky, A. and Kahneman, D. 1974).

The focus of this book, however, is not on what individuals should do, but in the context of this chapter, what people have a right to do. Wheeler argues that citizens should have the right and the means to overthrow totalitarian regimes. Let us assume that there are instances where rebels know that the criteria of "just rebellion theory" are satisfied. We might want them to rebel. However, is there any way to grant just these people the right to be armed and to rebel? I do not see how. As I explained in the previous chapter, rights are bestowed not on specific individuals, but on creatures with the relevant status or features: sentient creatures, sapient creatures, human beings, human beings over a certain age, citizens, and so forth. Once we grant a right, we must grant it to everyone with that status or those features. Given how often citizens mistakenly judge that their governments are totalitarian, we should be uneasy giving all adults both the rationale and the means to violently overthrow their governments. We could easily encourage the ouster of a legitimate regime. This is not idle speculation. A recent poll shows that 29% of Americans think we may soon need to violently overthrow the US government (Cassino, D. 2013). We should not be surprised. In 1861 segregationists had the means to rebel; they did just that. Timothy McVeigh had the means to attack a government he thought was coercive; he sincerely believed that blowing up the federal building in Oklahoma City was the first step in the necessary revolution; he believed that until he was executed (Michel, L. and Herbeck, D. 2002). Wheeler's argument will not be used to justify only what we, in retrospect, deem to be morally legitimate revolutions. His arguments will be used by segregationists and right-wing militia to "justify" *their* armed resistance; his proposed policies would ensure that they have the firepower to act on their beliefs. The fact that they are mistaken—and thus that their actions would be unjustified—would not diminish the misery they would cause. Nor would it alter the fact that, using Wheeler's reasoning, they have the right to be armed and, given their sincere beliefs, the right to use those weapons to rebel.

He can avoid this problem only by giving the government the authority to decide whether citizens' beliefs are rational. However, as he notes, that makes his proposal self-defeating since genuinely totalitarian regimes will always claim that potential rebels' judgments are misguided (1999: 115). It is difficult to see how he or we could give this right only to those who would be morally justified acting on it. Moreover, it is far from evident that giving this right to all citizens would be beneficial overall. Just look at three of the four examples he uses to support his claim that citizens should have the right and the means to effectively rebel.

Doubtless gun advocates will claim that I am playing fast and loose with the notion of rights—that I am making their exercise depend entirely on consequentialistic reasoning. I am not. Their objection conflates two distinct claims: (a) individuals can legitimately act on their rights only if the outcome is predictably beneficial; (b) we should grant or acknowledge a right only if we think doing so will be, overall, beneficial. The first claim is false; the second, true. When someone engages in free speech, we should (generally) not deny his exercise of the right simply because we think the outcome in his case would be detrimental. Rights limit our attempts to maximize the good. On the other hand, if we had clear evidence that *granting the right of free speech* were overall detrimental, then we would have good reason to not grant the right. Of course this is contrary to fact; Mill convincingly argues that the right to free speech is incredibly valuable even if some people's exercise of it is unfortunate. Likewise for other rights we prize. Whether the same is true for the right to bear arms is something pro-gun advocates must establish.

THREE IMPLICATIONS

There are three implications of Wheeler's view that many people—including many pro-gun advocates—would find worrisome. These are difficulties in addition to those just discussed and those mentioned in chapter 2.

One, if a government is likely to become totalitarian, given the power of their militaries, armed resistance is unlikely to succeed if citizens have only handguns and rifles. The rebels are more likely to succeed if they have mortars, bazookas, surface-to-air missiles, and so on. If Wheeler is convinced that there is a totalitarian regime lurking around every corner, then he should admonish citizens to acquire these larger firearms. Indeed, he should insist that people have rights to these weapons. Perhaps he would be happy to make this concession. Most of us would not be. Not even the other pro-gun advocates (Huemer, M. 2003: 323; Hunt, L. H. 2011: 118).

Two, if having an armed citizenry is essential for keeping governments from being or becoming totalitarian, then it seems that we should not simply *permit* citizens to keep firearms, we should *require* them to do so (although we might allow conscientious objection). The number of Americans who own guns is by all accounts declining and has been for some time. Wheeler might well contend that there are *enough* armed citizens to keep mischievous governments at bay. However, there must be a critical mass of armed citizens if they have any hope of success. So even if there are enough potential rebels now, there is a tipping point where the number of gun-owning citizens would be insufficient to the task. If so, then Wheeler seems to be committed to *requiring* people to own firearms, at least once that threshold has been met. I am unwilling to do that. I suspect few people are.

Three, and related to the previous point, if having "gun-ownership rights [is] a condition of the practical existence of other rights," then having a mere negative right—the right to own a gun if you can afford it—is insufficient to guarantee the "practical existence of other rights." If people must militarily thwart a totalitarian regime, they need firearms. If Wheeler thinks the right to defend oneself against totalitarian regimes would be empty without armed citizens, and a significant number of citizens cannot afford guns, then the state should tax the rich to finance firearms for the poor. Wheeler, and the other pro-gun advocates, would not find this option tolerable. They think gun rights are purely negative. They cannot have it both ways.

I now turn to discuss self-defense from individual attackers. As we will see, most problems that plagued Wheeler's view also plague this one. This one faces a few additional ones.

SELF-DEFENSE AGAINST INDIVIDUAL AGGRESSORS

All philosophical gun advocates argue that the right to bear arms stems, at least in part, from the right of self-defense against individual aggressors. Guns are a necessary or reasonable or effective means of self-defense against such people either within or away from one's home. To fully understand their views, we should determine what they mean by "means." However, since I want my evaluation to be applicable to all competing senses of "means," my comments will not be limited to a single view.

Whatever their account of means, all pro-gun advocates cite individual cases that they aver support their claims. Some, like Huemer's, are imaginary; others, like Hunt's, are actual.

Huemer defends his claim by describing two actions he thinks we will all agree are wrong; he claims both resemble gun bans. However, the first (confiscating someone's gun) does not so much resemble a gun ban as it is an instance of one. Perhaps, though, he was envisioning a case more like this: a killer breaks into someone's house and, before attacking the owner, steals his gun. This case is not an instance of a gun ban. However, this example puts the moral emphasis in the wrong place. What is wrong is the criminal's killing the victim; the stealing of the gun is a moral sideshow. So perhaps Huemer has something still different in mind. Joe goes to Ron's house to kill him. Just before he arrives, Bob goes into Ron's house and steals his gun. If that is what Huemer envisioned, the case is far-fetched. More relevant to the current discussion: it is subject to the same criticisms I raise to Huemer's second example.

This case (holding someone while another person stabs them) is not analogous to either a gun ban or serious, but less substantial, gun control. We know why that action is wrong. The agent is an accessory to murder. Looking at this dis-analogous case will not help us decide if gun control is acceptable.

Hunt focuses on a real case: the story of Florida resident John Lee. Lee claimed he was attacked without warning by three armed robbers outside his apartment as he was getting out of his car. He reportedly saved his life by whipping out a pistol and returning fire (Hunt, L. H. 2016: 38-40; Hunt, L. H. 2011: 116–122, 127). Hunt contends that Lee's gun was a *vital means* of self-defense (I will use this phrase to cover competing views of "means"). Without his gun, Lee would have died. Hunt thinks Lee's case is instructive. As he expresses it elsewhere, since modern guns are "precision instruments" (2016: 1055), we can grant people a right to bear arms knowing that if they follow simple rules, it would be "impossible" for them to harm anyone unintentionally.

Hunt's argument faces problems similar to those plaguing Wheeler. We will plausibly assume that an individual should guide her behavior by what I will call "just self-defense theory"—which resembles just war theory and what I earlier dubbed "just rebellion theory." The first criterion (just cause) may not always be satisfied since people can feel threatened even if they are not threatened. However, a violent response is justified only if the other is "an *actual* threat" (Uniacke, S. 1996: 162; emphasis in original). Minimally, the potential victim should *reasonably believe* that she is threatened.

The potential victim should also have reason to think (1) there are no viable options for protecting herself or avoiding harm; (2) there is a reasonable chance that her resistance will succeed; and (3) in defending herself, she will not impose excessive risks on others. Unfortunately, the potential victim can rarely be confident that she will succeed, at least not without putting others at risk. Among other things, a potential victim can make an otherwise innocuous (or minor) encounter threatening by responding as if it were threatening. This is the most charitable reading of events that led George Zimmerman to kill Treyvon Martin in 2012 (Fulton, S. and Martin, T. 2017).

What happens if we use these criteria to assess the Lee case? One, I find it odd that multiple robbers would shoot at a distant target unannounced. If they did, why did Lee infer that they were robbers rather than assassins? I would be shocked were there not other factors at play. For instance, it seems reasonable to think that *if* they were robbers and *if* they fired without warning, it was likely because they had good reason to think that Lee was armed. If so, then arguably Lee's gun was the reason he was shot, even if it might also have been the reason he was not killed given that he was shot.

This case also reveals the problem with Hunt's contention that guns are precision instruments. A firearm may be a precise weapon in the hands of a well-trained marksman, in non-stressful circumstances, when the target is close and in plain sight, and if there is no one else around who might be harmed by stray or ricocheting bullets. Lee's case is not at all like this. We do not know if he was trained. We do know that circumstances were highly stressful. We know he fired in what he thought was the general direction of the aggressors. How do these factors complicate our evaluation of what happened?

One, the robbers' would likely respond in kind. Two, we can infer that he shot quickly and repeatedly in an arc ("the attackers are somewhere over there"). Having a gunfight in the middle of an apartment complex parking lot—when one of the people is firing at no determinative target—could easily cause others serious harm. *This* is not an instance of precisely using an instrument.

Of course, we can safely assume that anyone who uses firearms in what she deems self-defense believes she is being attacked and believes she will succeed in stopping that attack. She might believe her actions won't harm anyone else. However, it is not enough that having a gun *would be* her best means of self-defense. It is not enough for her to sincerely believe that it would be. She must reasonably believe she is genuinely threatened and she has a reasonable chance of thwarting the threat without harming innocent others. That will not be easy to establish.

Until now we have been asking how individuals should respond to perceived threats. The issues are more complex when deciding if people have a serious right to bear arms.

Is there a Means Right to Own a Gun?

This brings us to the core question animating this book: Should people have a serious right to have and carry arms? This is not a question about the prudence or morality of any given individual's actions. Those questions arise along the fourth and fifth continua described in chapter 1. The issue here concerns the first three policy continua: whether we should grant (certain) individuals the right to bear (certain) arms, and whether (and how) we should regulate the arms people can legitimately own. Deciding that it is prudent or moral for an individual to defend herself will not straightforwardly reveal whether we should recognize a right to bear arms. Especially since this is a means right. It is not enough that bearing arms is occasionally beneficial. Owning firearms should *generally be* a vital means to achieving a valuable end. The grounds for the right evaporate if the means do not generally promote that end, or if in so doing, it risks significant harm to others.

Hunt disagrees. He criticizes this contention in two ways. One, he claims that it would not matter if statistics showed that granting unfettered private gun ownership harmed more people than it benefited. He asserts that such a statistical probability would be irrelevant *to me* if I know that I am a person "to whom these statistical considerations do not apply" (Hunt, L. H. 2016: 101). However, this response assumes more people have more self-knowledge than they have; it misunderstands what statistical evidence is and what it shows; it ignores the reams of evidence about the myriad ways in which we all overestimate own abilities, traits, tendencies, and the degree to which we misjudge how we will behave in future circumstances (Dunning, D. 2005; Dunning, D., Heath, C. and Suls, J. M. 2005; Ehrlinger, J., Gilovich, T. and Ross, L. 2005; Nickerson, R. S. 1998; Pronin, E. 2009; Pronin, E., Lin, D. Y. and Ross, L. 2002; LaFollette, H. 2017). No one who drives drunk or plays Russian roulette or goes canoeing in rapids thinks that she will be killed or harmed in so doing. If she did, then she would avoid those actions. She may know the statistical probabilities of being harmed; she is just confident that she is an exception. Even if Hunt were right that *some* people do *know* that they are exceptions, far more people wrongly believe that they are.

Two, Hunt avers we have good grounds for claiming firearms are a vital means to self-defense without having to worry about the empirical evidence. "[C]ommon sense and anecdotal evidence are ... sufficient to support this assertion that [from earlier in the paragraph] .... a gun can be an effective means of self-defense" (2016: 815). If we interpret this to mean simply that a gun is sometimes an effective means of self-defense, that claim is true. I say as much in chapter 2. However, Hunt is not repeating my uncontroversial claim. His assertion appears in the context of a long argument that we have a stringent right to own and carry guns since they are the most reasonable means of self-defense (2016: 767–926). This is a mistake.

We cannot rationally assess a complicated causal claim about the relative benefits and costs of private gun ownership by relying on anecdotes and common sense. The powers of selective attention and our susceptibility to the availability heuristic are too powerful. There are anecdotes aplenty, whether one is pro-gun or pro-control. If accurately and fully described, these may reveal what can happen; none are sufficient to reveal what is generally true. "Common sense" fares no better. I grew up hearing how common sense showed seat belts did not save lives (they cost them); leaded gasoline was safe ("what's the fuss?"); and the assertion that laws could promote workers safety was bureaucratic mumbo-jumbo. I eventually learned to be skeptical of so-called common sense. I remain so. What passes for common sense is often ill-informed prejudice (Rosenfeld, S. 2011).

Pro-gun advocates might acknowledge the force of my arguments but contend that they do not need to rely on Hunt's arguments above. They claim to have compelling empirical evidence of the benefits of owning and carrying guns. I explain and evaluate that research over the next three chapters. Here, I simply note that although these philosophers assert that they have compelling evidence, their use of it is insufficient to the argumentative task.

All the philosophers I discussed repeatedly cite the works of Gary Kleck and John Lott Jr. These authors purportedly offer empirical evidence of guns' benefits. However, these pro-gun philosophers simply rehearse these social scientists' conclusions. They make no attempt to explain how these authors reach their conclusions, nor do they critically assess their claims. Moreover, they appear oblivious to the work of the majority of social scientists who criticize the evidence offered by the academic demi-gods of the pro-gun movement. Hunt does cite one pro-gun advocate's views, but only as that view is *described by Kleck* rather than by the author himself (2016: 57). He does so at considerable cost. Had he read Cook, he would have seen that Cook was being facetious: he was trying to identify the problems plaguing Kleck's methodology (Cook, P. J. and Ludwig, J. 1996). Additionally, both Hunt and Huemer mention the National Crime Victimization Study, which is cited favorably by many pro-control advocates. However, their discussions do not reflect any deep familiarity with it. They simply repeat Kleck's complaints about it (Hunt, L. H. 2016: 852–859; Huemer, M. 2003: 314–315). That is not acceptable, although to their credit, they do at least mention some competing studies.

We need to understand the competing empirical evidence. That requires perusing the original literature. I discuss that literature over the next three chapters. Before I do, I want to first identify some worrisome implications of and tensions in the argument that guns are vital means of self-defense.

Three Implications

There are three worrisome implications of their views and arguments; two of these resemble implications of Wheeler's argument.

One, if multiple assailants attack a lone victim, then a handgun may be insufficient to thwart the attack, especially if the victim has less than stellar aim. In these admittedly rare cases, armed resistance is more likely to succeed if citizens have mortars or bazookas. If these philosophers want to ensure that individuals can always protect themselves from attack, then they should permit citizens to acquire larger firearms. Since they do not permit this, then these cases, however rare, would be what they elsewhere describe as instances of "preventing the prevention of a death . . . [This] is about as serious a wrong as killing" (Huemer, M. 2003: 307–308). This is the first hint of a pervasive tension pervading their arguments.

Two, if owning a gun is a vital means of self-defense, then one needs not only a negative right to bear arms she also needs a gun. A bare negative right is worthless. Therefore, if the philosopher's central moral interest is that people be able to defend themselves, and they believe that guns are a vital means to that end, then they should advocate a positive right to a gun. The state should provide guns for anyone who does not have and cannot afford one. However, the authors expressly reject such a right (Hall 2006: 294; Hunt 2011: 116). That undermines their claim to be principally concerned that individuals be able to defend themselves. It suggests they are more committed to the theoretical position that the only, or by far the most serious, rights are negative. This is the second hint of a pervasive tension.

Three, pro-gun advocates talk as if all aggressors were established criminals and their victims were standardly law-abiding citizens. Some expressly say just that. Arguments for gun control "amount to arguing that the self-defense rights of noncriminal gun owners are overridden by the state's need to protect society from criminal gun owners" (Huemer, M. 2003: 308). However, unless one uses the phrase "noncriminal" (or law-abiding) ambiguously, this is misleading or demonstrably false. Of course, we sometimes have to worry about attacks from criminals. However, we must also worry about attacks from acquaintances, friends, family, and lovers. In the United States, half of all people killed are killed by an acquaintance; more than 15% are killed by a family member; women are most commonly killed by a spouse or lover (Federal Bureau of Investigation 2017; Khazan, O. 2017). Consequently, if we wish to promote public safety, the issue is not simply how to keep guns out of the hands of criminals, we should find ways to protect the public from predictable harm that follows from having more or less unlimited private ownership of guns. This is related to the tension that infuses their views.

A Pervasive Tension

All the philosophers advocating a serious right to bear arms support some forms of gun control along the three policy continua identified in chapter 1. Several want to limit *who* can own guns; most want to limit *which* guns people can own. Given their acceptance of restrictions along these first two continua, they must also accept some regulations to ensure that the limits on the first two continua are satisfied. Let me explain why these acknowledgements do not sit comfortably with many of their claims and arguments.

THE FIRST CONTINUUM: WHO CAN OWN GUNS?

Three pro-gun philosophers expressly acknowledge that we should limit some people from owning guns. Huemer claims that mentally stable, noncriminal adults have the right to bear arms; he thereby implies that children, criminals, and mentally ill people do not (Huemer, M. 2003: 324; Hunt, L. H. 2016: 138). Wheeler adds one additional qualification: only those "who are properly trained in firearms" have this right (Wheeler, S. C., III 1999: 123). How do they defend these forms of gun control?

There is nothing unusual about wanting to keep guns out of the hands of some mentally ill people if one supports moderate gun control. Control advocates would support this restriction for the same reason that they support others: to protect the public from risky behavior. However, this is not a rationale that plays well with arguments advocates offer for a serious right to bear arms and against serious gun control. Since on their view this right is *very* stringent, why should mentally ill people be denied rights to enjoyment and means to self-defense? They have the same need for recreation as everyone else. They are as likely as other citizens to be harmed by roguish governments and private individuals. Gun advocates only plausible rationale for denying them the (or overriding their) right to bear arms is that these advocates think that the consequences of giving them his right would be deleterious.

I agree. However, I am unsure how *they* can make this argument. One, what evidence do they have supporting these suppositions about mentally ill people? Evidence suggests the answer is: very little (Swanson, J. W. and Robertson A. G., 2013). Since the empirical evidence is missing, or perhaps contrary to their claims, I suspect they are relying on armchair arguments about people's motivations, character, and behavior. On my view, that is acceptable. However, as we have seen, they eschew armchair arguments when these show that and why widespread private ownership of guns is dangerous to others. Why should they accept just *this* armchair argument? Two, given their proclivity to embrace Nozickian-like views of inviolable rights, this does not seem like a plausible argument. I doubt they have or could have evidence that the degree of *additional* harm these people would perpetrate—compared with an average gun owner—is sufficient to override such a stringent right. As Huemer states: people's rights to recreation (and presumably self-defense) can be overridden only if the harms are "many times greater than the benefits" (2003: 297). How can they meet this demanding standard?

What about former violent felons? Gun advocates could claim it is just too risky to let them own guns. How, though, do *they* mount this argument? Former felons are as likely as the rest of us to be oppressed by totalitarian regimes and to be attacked by individual aggressors. Given gun advocates' claims about the stringency of the right of self-defense, I doubt they have or could obtain evidence that the harm these former offenders cause by owning guns is "many times greater" than the benefit of being able to defend themselves. I do not want these people owning guns. But then, I do not embrace gun advocates' views about the stringency of the right to bear arms.

Their second option would be to argue that these former felons *forfeited* their rights to own a gun. However, the notion of the forfeiture of rights is notoriously contentious. Moreover, that notion, inasmuch as it can be defended, seems applicable only when a person is under active criminal supervision. Once she has completed her sentence and "paid her debt to society," it is unclear why and how she continues to morally forfeit said rights, even if it is also true that she may have legally forfeited them (LaFollette, H. 2005). Finally, even if there were *some* rights that *some* former felons continue to forfeit upon release, why is owning a gun among them? Former felons still have rights of free speech, free religious expression, the right not to incriminate themselves, and the right not to be subject to cruel and unusual punishment. If out of all rights, the only one they forfeit is the right to bear arms, then it seems this right cannot be as stringent as these thinkers proclaim—or as a Nozickian theorist would surely aver.

THE SECOND CONTINUUM: WHICH GUNS CAN THEY OWN?
At least three of these thinkers acknowledge that we can justifiably limit private ownership of some types of firearms. People do not have rights to privately own grenades and bazookas (Hunt, L. H. 2011: 118), nuclear weapons (that would be "absurd") (Huemer, M. 2003: 323), or motorized artillery (Hall, T. 2006: 295).

They claim that the suggestion that anyone should be permitted to own such weapons is ludicrous. I agree, as would anyone who supports moderate gun control. However, it is not clear how they could embrace these claims.

Pro-gun advocates assert it is not dangerous for law-abiding citizens to own handguns or rifles. If they are correct, why should they fear letting these citizens own bazookas? If, as these advocates aver, only criminals commit crimes with handguns, rifles, or assault weapons (Huemer, M. 2003: 308), why do these philosophers seem to think that law-abiding citizens would morph into criminals if allowed to own a mortar?

Indeed, I would have thought that there would be fewer problems with law-abiding people owning heavy weapons. I suspect there might be fewer accidental deaths, suicides, or impulsive murders using these weapons. Fewer people would "play around" with heavy artillery. Few people would clean them and thus die when they accidentally discharge; few would stash them where unsuspecting children might find and abuse them; no one would keep them under her pillow for self-protection or carry them to work or while going out for a night on the town. Conversely, if we should fear bazooka-toting law-abiding citizens, then it seems we have even stronger reasons to fear that these people might use handguns for mischievous ends.

I would have also thought that larger weapons would be less commonly used offensively. It would be difficult to hide a bazooka under your trench coat as you enter the local 7-Eleven to rob it or when approaching tourists walking down the street.

Of course people armed with bazookas and mortars may kill more people than someone armed with automatic handguns or rifles—although that is not *obviously* true (it would be harder to sneak them into a mall, theater, or school). However, even if it were true, given advocates' arguments about the stringency of the right to bear arms, the burden of proof is on them to show why the cost of allowing citizens to own these heavy weapons is "many times greater" than the benefits to the owners gained from recreation, self-protection, and the ability to resist totalitarian regimes.

THE THIRD CONTINUUM: HOW THEY CAN BE OWNED, TRANSFERRED, AND SO ON

Since all these pro-gun thinkers expressly accept limits along one— or both—of the first two continua, then they would need to accept restrictions on guns to ensure that the wrong people do not obtain the wrong weapons. These restrictions are possible only if the government has a robust form of registration supported by rigorous background checks. The government would need an up-to-date national database to ensure the person purchasing or acquiring the weapon is qualified. There must also be mechanisms to identify and punish people who flout these legal regulations.

Why Are These Problems?

Pro-gun advocates send mixed messages. On the one hand, they recognize that some people should not be allowed to obtain any guns and there are some guns that no one should be allowed to obtain. These are open admissions, stated nonchalantly. On the other hand, they dismiss, lambaste, and belittle pro-control arguments, even though these arguments appeal to the same considerations they use to deny any guns to the mentally ill and heavy weapons to any people. As stated, this is not *quite* an outright contradiction. However, it sure flirts with it. It is difficult, if not impossible, to reconcile the stark differences in the content and tone of these respective stances. Either pro-gun arguments fail to successfully defend the forms of control they accept, or, if their defense of these forms of control is plausible, they seem to acknowledge the force of arguments that justify more extensive gun control.

CONCLUSION

Gun advocates most plausible argument for a serious right to bear arms is to show that privately owning guns is a vital means to achieving a significant fundamental end (security) without excessive costs. So the plausibility of their rights claim depends—much to their chagrin—on a careful examination of the empirical evidence. In chapter 6, I describe the available evidence; in the following chapter, I evaluate it. But first, in chapter 5, I identify the obstacles to attaining empirical evidence. I also explain ways that we might obtain it.

Looking for Empirical Evidence

In the second chapter, I argued that the armchair arguments tilt in favor of moderate—and perhaps even serious—gun control. In chapter 3, I argued that there is no reason to think there is a fundamental right to bear arms. Although there are some reasons to think there might be a derivative right, even the US Supreme Court decision hailed by pro-gun advocates states that that right is not especially stringent; it does not rule out a range of current and prospective gun control measures. I explained why the proffered philosophical arguments for a serious right to bear arms are compatible with—indeed demand—some gun control. In short, every line of argument I have examined supports at least moderate gun control. It seems the contentious issue is not whether we should recognize a serious right to bear arms, but whether there are compelling reasons for serious gun control.

Perhaps, though, I am jumping the argumentative gun. There could be solid empirical evidence of profound benefits and few costs of the private ownership of guns, evidence that would tip the justificatory scales in the opposite direction. This could provide a direct (albeit not rights-based) argument for a serious claim to bear arms. It might also show that the right to own guns is a morally demanding means right. Therefore, exploring the empirical evidence is the next step in our quest to resolve this issue.

The search for empirical evidence will take us over familiar terrain, albeit seen from a different perspective. In discussing the armchair arguments, we asked about the potential benefits (self-defense against tyrannical governments and individual aggressors) and potential costs (increases in homicides, accidental deaths, suicides, serious injuries, and armed robberies) of the extensive private ownership of guns. We discussed these issues again when assessing claims about a putative serious right to bear arms, primarily because the most plausible form of these arguments depends on the claim that owning guns is an especially effective means of self-defense. To that extent, the arguments here and the next two chapters will look familiar. We want to ascertain if we have, and if not, how we might obtain, empirical evidence bolstering or undermining the armchair arguments or arguments for a derivative right to bear arms.

WHY IT IS DIFFICULT TO FIND RELIABLE EMPIRICAL EVIDENCE

Some pro-gun advocates think that empirical evidence on gun control is not only available but irresistible; the inferences from it, incontrovertible. Lance Stell avers that the evidence is *so* clear that gun control advocates "must be embarrassed" for not recognizing or acknowledging the plain truth in front of their faces.

What is this overwhelming evidence? Here is how he puts it:

> These data show long-term non-association between America's homicide rate and America's concomitant, steady increase in guns per 100,000 population over the century. Non-association between variation in the homicide rate and variation (always increasing) in society's gun aggregate rules out social causation. (2001: 30)

Put differently, this data shows that there has been an increase in the total number of privately owned guns during the same time that there has been a decrease in homicides. Stell asserts that the conjunction of these two facts "rules out" the possibility that private ownership of guns causes an increase in homicides. Gary Kleck employs the same argument (1997/2006: 18), although he does not state it so boldly.

The argument fails. The main flaw arises from Stell's claim that the data "rules out" the possibility that an increase in guns could increase homicides. That is the issue on which I focus. However, I first mention an important methodological question that could easily get forgotten: Is his data accurate? I suspect the homicide data is based on CDC and FBI data; therefore, it is certainly reliable and likely true; I explain why later. His claim about the number of guns is plausible, although not as secure as the first claim since we lack an authoritative mechanism for determining how many guns people hold privately. I do not wish to challenge his data; I am merely emphasizing that a causal claim can be no more plausible than the data on which it rests. Even if we accept Stell's data, we should understand that not all data is equally reliable.

Stell's principal error is in inferring that since two phenomena are not positively correlated, then the first *cannot* cause the second. Argument over; case closed. However, the data does not rule out causation since his argument avoids, ignores, or masks three critical facts that inform a more plausible interpretation of the evidence.

One, although the total stock of guns in the United States (and thus, the *average* number of guns per person) *has* increased, over the same period the *percentage* of the population owning guns has decreased from 47% to 31% (Tavernise, S. and Gebeloff, R. 2013; General Social Survey 2015: 1). When trying to ascertain if there is a causal correlation between guns and homicides, arguably the relevant statistic is the percentage of people who have ready access to guns, not the total number of privately owned guns.

Two, Stell apparently is not aware that during the decade with an appreciable increase in the number of guns—albeit in fewer hands—there has been a significant increase (50%) in the number of *gunshot injuries* (Fields, G. and McWhirter, C. 2012). If we read the data as straightforwardly as Stell does, that would show that more guns, more gunshot injuries. However, concluding that the increase in the number of guns caused the increase in gunshot injuries would be premature. Looking at two data points is never sufficient to establish a causal relationship. That said, we should ask: What could have led to the increase in woundings? The increase in the number of guns could partly explain the phenomena, either directly or indirectly. However, I would be shocked if it were the only factor.

Three, given this increase, we should ascertain why fewer people died from their wounds. Perhaps gun owners have increasingly worse aim, they have better aim and are trying not to kill the people they shoot, or they have become systematically luckier. None of those explanations is plausible. The most sensible explanation was offered by the *Wall Street Journal*: we now have better equipped emergency rooms, with more and better trained trauma surgeons, and—partly because we have become more urbanized—society has improved the means and speed of transporting gunshot victims to trauma centers. These factors explain why we now save many people who would have previously died from their injuries (Fields, G. and McWhirter, C. 2012).

All of a sudden, the correlation Stell thought provided an open-and-shut case for pro-gun advocates is not in the least convincing. Although more guns may be correlated with fewer homicides, the explanation of that phenomenon is rather different from the one he advanced. This case illustrates an important fact about scientific investigation: data does not interpret itself. We need armchair arguments, shaped by informed background empirical knowledge, to infuse and inform our reading and interpretation of data.

The Scientific Problem

We should not be too critical of Stell. Many of us are duped by statistics. To intellectually vaccinate ourselves from their misguided or insidious uses (Huff, D. 1993/1954), we must understand what scientists seek in their experiments, why it is difficult for them to succeed, and how even well-intended statistical manipulation can go awry. Standardly, when scientists investigate a phenomenon they want to identify causal relationships. If they can discover what causes what, it helps us understand what happened. That empowers us to predict what will happen and then act accordingly. For instance, astronomers predicted the precise time and location of the solar eclipse that occurred while I was completing this chapter. With this information at hand, citizens could make intelligent decisions about whether, when, and where to go if they wanted to witness this rare celestial event. Likewise, if we know that asbestos causes cancer, we now know not to install asbestos insulation in our houses, and we know to remove it from existing buildings. And were we to learn that allowing people to carry handguns lowered crime and homicides, then we would have good reason to permit people to be armed.

When scientists conduct these inquiries, they are not trying to make specific causal claims: whether Ralph divorced Ron *because* Ron had an affair, whether Judy lost her job *because* she criticized her boss, or whether Phillip was acquitted *because* his dad bribed two jurors. Scientists look for general causal claims: Does lead in the atmosphere diminish people's brain function? Does exposure to benzene (a by-product of smoking and internal combustion engines) cause cancer? Does a diet high in saturated fats cause heart disease? Does exercise prolong a person's life? Or, to take our current issue, does an increased presence of guns diminish or increase crime or homicide? Although there are similarities between the specific and general inquiries, they are not identical. The problems facing specific causal claims are occasionally daunting; generally, however, they are piddling when compared to those we face when trying to establish more general causal claims.

The history of science shows us why we should be cautious when attributing causes (hereafter understood as general causes). That history is littered with examples where prominent scientists reached what we now know to be seriously misguided conclusions. Well into the 1400s many scientists still embraced the Ptolemaic view of the universe (Kuhn, T. 1962: esp. chap. 8–10). Until the late 1800s, scientists thought light traveled through an invisible luminiferous ether that pervaded our universe (Michelson, A. A. and Morley, E. W. 1887). Well into the 1950s, scientists were confident that smoking did not cause cancer (Northrup, E. 1957). In retrospect we see that these scientists, although wrong, were neither silly nor insincere. Their claims *at the time* were plausible.

To understand how they went wrong, and how we might do better, we must think carefully about how we can experimentally confirm causal claims. Specifying reliable experimental strategies will take us down serpentine methodological and historical paths. I begin by briefly asking: (1) Whom do researchers study? (2) What do they want to know about these subjects? The answers vary depending on the issue they are investigating. If they are trying to isolate factors that exacerbate diabetes, they will not study the same people—or want to know the same things about the people—as they would if they were studying sexual behavior, Parkinson's disease, or defensive gun uses.

Who and What to Study

FINDING THE APPROPRIATE SUBJECTS

No experiment can succeed if the researcher studies the wrong subjects. If we are trying to determine if guns are effective means of self-defense, researchers will not study only ministers, marathoners, or mechanics—although, of course, a well-designed study might discover that these groups have an especially high rate of victimization or are more likely to use guns defensively. If that is what experimenters find, then that information will guide future research. However, barring such a finding, researchers beginning a study would not limit their scrutiny to these groups. Or if they do, we know the study is a waste of time and money.

If we could do so easily, we would study everyone who has used a gun defensively, everyone person who owns a gun, or everyone who has been the victim of gun violence. The problem, of course, is that that we do not know who these people are prior to research. The only way to be certain that we have studied all members of the target population (the people we wish to study) is to study the entire population. Assuming we could obtain accurate data—that the subjects would truthfully report their behavior and others actions—then we would know who owns firearms, who *tried* to use them defensively, who used them aggressively, who committed suicide with them, and who was killed accidentally by them. With this data to hand, we could plausibly discern the benefits and costs of private gun ownership.

The problem is that no studies include *everyone*. Although admirably thorough, even major studies conducted by the Census Bureau or the FBI inevitably let a few subjects slip through the experimental cracks. With the exception of efforts to study everyone, the prudent strategy is to study a representative group (the subject class) of the entire group we are studying (the target class). If the subject class is not representative of the target class, researchers cannot reliably generalize findings in subjects to the target population. This is easily seen with surveys. If the only people the Gallup organization polled in the 2016 presidential race were those with "Hilary Clinton for President" yard signs, then the study's results would have been useless in predicting the eventual outcome of that race. If public health researchers examined data only from areas known to have a high (or low) incidence of private gun ownership, then their findings would not provide solid guidance in establishing any connection between the private ownership of guns and either successful defensive gun uses or gun homicides, suicides, or accidents. Barring sheer luck, choosing unrepresentative subjects skews experimental findings.

The scientific problem is that often we do not know in advance who is representative. In the absence of such knowledge, the proper approach is to use an adequately sized random sample of the target population (all people with diabetes, all people who carry guns, all people with emphysema, etc.). Scientists plausibly assume that an adequately sized, truly random subject class will be statistically likely to represent the target class. Therefore, findings in the subject class can be safely generalized to the entire target class. Randomness is not intrinsically valuable; it is a valuable methodological means to an experimental end.

WHAT TO KNOW ABOUT THESE SUBJECTS

It is not enough to examine the appropriate subjects; we must obtain the relevant information from and about them. The problem, as we shall see more clearly later, is that we often do not know what *is* relevant. Even if we do know that some feature is relevant, we may not know the ways that and the degree to which it is. Relevance is something we typically discover only after conducting research. Initial research may give us a glimpse of what factors are relevant; that information can then guide later research.

When we are unsure which features are relevant, a prudent option is to note factors that we know are relevant in other experimental contexts. These include general information about subjects: age, gender, socioeconomic status, and the environment in which they live (urban, rural, suburban, etc.). If we are conducting studies to inform gun control policies, then we need information specifically relevant to that inquiry: who owns how many guns; and whether they have used guns offensively or defensively or had guns used against them.

The Search for a Gold Standard

With these broad guidelines in hand, how can researchers find relevant and complete (comprehensive) data that allows them to identify a general causal relationship? Scientists have a methodological Holy Grail, an empirical design they pursue, even if they never fully attain it. The researcher's gold standard is a scrupulously designed, judiciously overseen, adequately sized, double-blind experiment with randomly selected subjects, assigned randomly to study or control groups.

Scientists choose subjects randomly to increase the chance that they represent the target class; the experiment should be double blind to eliminate any placebo effect. After conducting the study, researchers look for statistically significant correlations between features of the subjects studied, correlations that might warrant an inference that an event or confluence of events caused a particular effect. Not just any correlation will do. It should meet the .05 confidence level, that is, the correlation should be sufficiently strong so that the probability that the results could have occurred by chance is 5% or less.

For example, we could test a new drug by randomly dividing people with lupus into two groups, administer a promising drug to half and a placebo to the other half. Neither the subjects nor the researchers would know who gets the drug and who gets the placebo until the study is completed. The experiment is instructive if researchers find that the group receiving the drug had statistically fewer lupus symptoms compared to the placebo group. Experiments can also be instructive when they "fail"; they may force medical researchers to reassess their previous belief (or hope) that a drug will be efficacious and safe in treating lupus.

It is sensible to think that experiments so designed and executed would produce reliable results. The problem is that it is difficult, if not impossible, to meet such rigorous conditions. Even if we try to meet them, the standard is not always golden. Drug safety and efficacy studies—where researchers are most likely to hew to the standard— are not foolproof. Years after the Food and Drug Administration (FDA) approves a drug, physicians may discover that medication has injurious (or more injurious) side effects than researchers had found in clinical trials. Some medications were used for more than half a century before we recognized their deleterious side effects (ProCon. org 2014).

Ways Studies Go Awry

How could studies so designed go awry? Generally we assume that the researchers are looking at and for relevant information, and that the data they collect is accurate. Unfortunately, in the early stages of scientific discovery, researchers do not know which subjects are worthy of study and which features of those subjects are scientifically relevant. Much of medical history is an attempt to isolate who and what are medically relevant. Ideas that are now old hat were not only unknown, they would have been thought to be absurd. For most of human history, physicians thought disease was caused by bad humors, demonic possession, and so forth. It was not until the mid-1800s that physicians and researchers on the forefront of scientific medicine recognized that germs were the culprit. Prior to that discovery, surgeons did not wash their hands before surgery. After all, they could not imagine any reason for doing so. We now know that a surgeon's washing her hands before a procedure exponentially increases the chance that her patients will survive (Harvard University Library Open Collections 2017).

One instructive story concerns Hungarian physician Ignaz Semmelweiss who, in the 1840s, was the director of the maternity clinic in a Vienna hospital. One ward of his clinic had an unusually high death rate. He assumed there had to be an explanation; his hunch reflects the core impulse driving science: things happen for a reason. However, not only did he not have an explanation, he was unsure what might count as an explanation. He initially explored all options, including ones that now seem ludicrous. For instance, he had the hospital priest change the direction in which he walked through the ward (Hempel, C. G. 1966: chap. 2.1). As bizarre as this now seems, when you do not have the slightest idea why the death rate is higher in one ward, a curious researcher will explore all options in hopes of eventually discovering the cause (Nuland, S. 2004). After all, the correct explanation—invisible life forms—would have seemed equally far-fetched. Even those in the hospital who were skeptical adopted his proposals. Physicians washed their hands before and after surgery and between exams with chlorinated lime. The results were immediate and dramatic. It took some time before his ideas were widely accepted. Now this is a truism we learned from our parents and in elementary school.

This story is not unique. Well into the 1900s medical investigators were unsure about causal facts we now take for granted. Until then, much of modern medicine was consumed with identifying the causes of, and eventually cures for, infectious diseases. Into the twentieth century, these were the primary culprits explaining humans' relatively brief lifespan. However, as increased sanitary measures—and later vaccinations—led to a noticeable decline in early deaths (McKeown, T. 1976), people who lived longer began to develop previously unknown, or at least rare, diseases. The major culprit: heart disease. Physicians and researchers sought to understand why some people were more likely to develop heart disease. Initially they did not know where to look; they did not know what was medically relevant. This prompted the development of the legendary Framingham study, first conceptualized in the 1940s and initiated the following decade.

Over the years, physicians identified factors in their patients that seemed most commonly associated with cardiovascular disease. It seemed more common in males, people with elevated blood pressures, people with high blood cholesterol, people with long and frequent use of alcohol and cigarettes, people who were overweight, and it was inversely correlated with people who were physically active. The researchers assumed some number of these factors helped explain heart disease. What they did not know was whether these factors were accidentally correlated with an increased chance of heart disease or if they were causal factors, and if they were, whether they were connected with or independent of one another.

They tested and followed 6,000 people from the town of Framingham, Massachusetts. They did detailed family histories, social histories (including habits), and regular physical exams and blood work on the subjects. They followed these patients for up to forty years (Framingham Heart Study 2016). The hope was that this longitudinal study would reveal the primary causes of heart disease. Once they had identified the causes, then physicians would have an idea about how to reverse or treat the problem.

The study yielded significant results. They *mostly* verified the previous hunches about possible causal factors, even if researchers remained unclear about which factors were especially important. Many of those study's results still stand. However, some have been challenged; most have been tweaked. For instance, researchers began to notice that not all cholesterol is created equal. While elevated low-density lipoproteins are a detrimental form of cholesterol, high-density lipoproteins are not only not detrimental, they counteract the effects of low-density lipoproteins. Others discovered the significant role of triglycerides in heart disease.

After the study's initial reports, other researchers tried to determine what caused high cholesterol, especially low-density lipoproteins. What contributes to increased weight? Is it just calories? Are all calories created equally? Or do so some (saturated fats and sugar) get converted to body fat more quickly than others (mono-saturated fats)? We now have some answers, but investigations continue and will continue into the foreseeable future. With each new discovery, researchers often identify a new relevant factor or they learned that some factor was more or less relevant than they previously thought. This history illustrates just how difficult it is to make informed causal claims.

Consider the drug studies to which I earlier alluded. These seem to be especially amenable to scientific investigation. They usually seek to meet the scientific gold standard. Since they divided the subject class randomly, it appears that those being studied were relevant. Since the researchers employed a double-blind methodology, there is little chance that some extraneous factors taint their findings. We must assume that those collecting the data were well-intentioned and careful. Therefore, the data should be accurate. So how could they go wrong as often as they did?

I suspect there are two related problems. One, since the probability of negative side effects from pharmaceuticals is often small, the researchers do not study enough subjects to identify these rare events. Two, there are too many potential confounding factors—seemingly minor conditions than might alter the drug's absorption and its effects. Here are just a few of those factors: (a) genetics: some people may be genetically inclined to be especially sensitive to certain compounds; (b) gender: we know that some conditions—and some negative reactions—are more likely to appear in one gender, perhaps because of the drug's interactions with gender-specific hormones; (c) other medications: the new pharmaceutical might have more negative effects when taken in concert with some individual or collection of medications; (d) other medical conditions: a medication that may work just fine on someone with *just* elevated cholesterol may have deleterious side effects if the person also has type 2 diabetes. We could go on. The researchers can control only for factors that they know—or reasonably believe to be—relevant. What *is* relevant is something that continually emerges from ongoing research.

Special Problems with Public Policy Issues

Although biomedical experiments tend to be more susceptible to rigorous testing, the previous examples reveal myriad ways in which they may misfire. In contrast, public policy issues, which are the focus of this book, are neither practically nor morally amenable to this degree of control and manipulation (Wellford, C. F., Pepper, J. V., and Petrie, C. V. 2004). Just how safe—or dangerous—are nuclear power plants, high-voltage transmission lines, or texting on cell phones while driving? Sometimes we do not know which factors are relevant and how we might investigate them. Moreover, key phrases like "safe" and "risky" are vague. Almost anything we do has *some* associated risks. How much risk is too much? Judgments of safety and risk are always comparative: How risky is some action *relative to alternatives*?

Consider the current issue. It is practically impossible and morally objectionable to try to meet the scientific gold standard when researching private gun ownership. We would have to identify a randomly selected group of adults, divide them into subject and control groups, give members of the subject class a firearm, and ask members of the control group who currently have firearms to surrender them . . . and promise not to obtain another. We would have to randomly select the groups and ensure that each group is sufficiently large to "cancel" any complicating personal characteristics or environmental circumstances that might influence the outcome (did they live in equally high-crime-rate areas, were members of the household mentally ill or have a criminal past, etc.?). Then we would have to follow subjects for several years to identify the consequences of privately owning (various kinds of) firearms, especially given the different ways that people store them and whether they carry them. Practically, we cannot employ a double-blind methodology since both subjects and researchers will know if they have a gun. Even if we could surmount these monumental methodological problems, such studies would be morally abhorrent. It would require forcing some people to own guns they do not want and to deny guns to some who do. For this issue, we must set our empirical sights lower.

Even so, we know we should look for relevant, comprehensive, and accurate data, interpret that data appropriately, and then draw plausible inferences. Each step must be informed by careful armchair arguments. A misstep at any point will taint the findings. What are our options when studying complex social phenomena? Significant social effects usually result from multiple interacting causes, typically from a disjunction of conjunctively sufficient conditions. For instance, gun violence might be caused by factors a, b, and c; or b, d, and f; or c, g, and h, and so forth. To make matters scientifically messier, there are often multiple *dependent* causes of crime and violence, for example, poverty, urbanization, intelligence, education, and health, and so on. Awareness of these obstacles must inform our inquiry.

OPTIONS FOR OBTAINING EMPIRICAL EVIDENCE

There are three types of experimental methodologies we might use. There are also three potential sources of data. The problem is, although these two sets of considerations overlap, neither neatly maps onto the other, although there is some overlap. I hope to describe both in ways that are illuminating without being confusing.

Three Methodologies

Researchers might employ three different research methodologies. My categorization of these slightly differs from ones often used. Although not a lot hangs on it, I think my scheme allows me to draw some methodological distinctions that better describe and evaluate various forms of gun research. The three approaches: case control studies, epidemiological studies, and surveys. All methods have a common overarching aim: to discover causal connections, although they use *somewhat* different methodological means to achieve these common research ends.

Case control studies are often treated in the literature as a form of epidemiological study. In them, researchers identify a small sample of cases with something in common, for example, they are all victims of homicide. Researchers then compare the findings in the subject class to a control group (non-victims). Members of the control group should be residents of the same city or residents of an economically, racially, educationally, and socially similar city. The researchers compare findings within each group to see if there are statistically relevant differences between them, differences that might explain differences in the phenomenon they are studying.

Epidemiological studies (as I use the term) examine data in larger populations (usually multiple cities, if not states or countries) to determine if two relevant factors are correlated in ways that suggest that one causes the other. Researchers usually use one of the two common sources of data I identify shortly to see if levels of gun ownership, or the frequency with which people carry guns in public, correlates with the number of defensive gun uses or with gun homicides, suicides, or accidents.

In the third form, researchers, or sometimes governmental agencies, survey people about various issues that might inform claims about the costs and benefits of private gun ownership. What distinguishes surveys from epidemiological studies is not that the latter uses individuals' self-reports while the former does not. Both must use self-reports. However, while in surveys the only sources of information are self-reports, in epidemiological studies, this is simply one information source. For instance, in the Framingham Heart Study, physicians would ask subjects about their diets or alcohol use. Researcher would pair these self-reports with independent evidence, for example, regular blood work and physical examinations.

All three methodologies can be valuable, although they have different roles and different strengths. Case control studies can expose profitable lines for further research, they can duplicate and thus support findings from others sources, and they can fill gaps and give more investigatory texture to findings from larger scale studies. However, their role is limited since they study a relatively small number of subjects within a confined geographical area.

Epidemiological studies are usually the richest sort of information. They often rely on data collected by research groups or, more commonly, governmental agencies (Wellford, C. F. et al. 2004: 22–30). They tend to study a significant number of subjects, sometimes the entire population. Often multiple researchers conduct the study and interpret the results. That explains why other researchers are more likely to take their findings seriously.

Surveys can also be valuable, especially larger surveys conducted by government agencies (like the National Crime Victimization Studies) and academic institutions or institutes. Surveys by individuals researchers, like Gary Kleck or Philip Cook, are also worth consideration. However, all surveys "share common methodological and survey sampling-related problems" (Wellford, C. F. et al. 2004: 35), problems on which I elaborate in the next section.

Three Sources of Data

The preceding section described the three main methodologies. Following are the four sources of data that researchers typically use. As I explained earlier, and as you doubtless noticed, scientists using some methodologies are more likely to use particular types of data. However, although there is some overlap, it is not complete. That is why I separate the discussions.

The sources are (1) official governmental data, which often include some significant portion of the population; (2) data produced by institutions or institutes; (3) data collected by individual researchers or teams; and (4) although this cuts across all of the above groups, surveys.

OFFICIAL GOVERNMENT DATA

Government data is generally more reliable than the alternatives. Since the number of subjects is usually high, the subject class more likely represents the target class. Moreover, they are often carefully designed and include internal controls that make it more likely that the data is accurate and appropriately catalogued. In the United States the FBI and the Department of Justice collect and compile crime data. The Centers for Disease Control and Prevention (CDC) collects health data, and, particularly relevant to the current inquiry, mortality and morbidity information. The Census Bureau collects and compiles general information about the familial, racial, economic, and social makeup of the US population.

Researchers for these agencies face a daunting task since the data is collected by different people, in different environments, and often by different institutions. Researchers at the national headquarters must find ways to ensure that the data from these myriad sources is comparable. For instance, there are 12,000 police departments in the United States who submit their data to the FBI. Each local jurisdiction makes an initial classification of each encounter with, and investigation by, local law enforcement with the relevant public. They summarize their initial findings, although they may later revise those if they uncover new evidence. The officer on the scene, the district attorney, the local clerk who combines individuals' reports, and the personnel in the national office who compile those reports from each jurisdiction must categorize each event. Was it an armed robbery or an attempted murder? Are the attacker and the victim acquainted or related? If so, how? Did the victim use a gun defensively? That may sound simple enough. However, what determines if an offender *uses* a gun? There are obvious cases. If the robber does not have a gun and does nothing that might lead a reasonable person to think she does, then we should not categorize the crime as one in which the assailant used a firearm. On the other hand, if she wields a gun and threatens the victim with it, then clearly she did use a gun while committing the crime. However, there are many possibilities between these extremes. What if the person had a gun but never brandished it? What if the victim saw a bulge in the assailant's coat and inferred that it was a gun? What if the criminal told the victim that he had a gun? How these crimes are classified will depend on a number of factors, including the questions the police ask, how the police phrase—and the order in which they ask—the questions, the tone in which they ask them, the state of the victim when questioned, and how the officer on the scene interprets the victim's response. It is implausible to assume that every officer in any jurisdiction, let alone every officer in every jurisdiction, handles interviews and interprets answers similarly. Hence, they are unlike to provide uniform categorization of criminal encounters.

Each jurisdiction then sends its data to the FBI and the Department of Justice who assemble the diverse reports, tabulate each jurisdiction's findings, and publish a summary report. These agencies work to ensure that altercations and crimes are classified similarly across all districts. It does not help if districts disagree about what counts as "assault with a deadly weapon," "attempted murder," "intent to harm," "successful defensive gun use," and so on. To lessen the chance of non-uniform data, the FBI distributes the *Uniform Crime Reporting Handbook* to all law enforcement departments specifying precisely how critical terms should be interpreted. This practice increases, but does guarantee, that they will obtain consistent data across geographically, political, and economically diverse jurisdictions. The *Handbook* begins with a plea to police departments that highlights the dangers the FBI seeks to avoid:

> Classifying and scoring offenses are the two most important functions that a participant in the UCR Program performs. The data that contributing agencies provide are based on these two functions, so scrupulous attention to the Program's guidelines helps to ensure accurate and reliable data. (Federal Bureau of Investigation 2016: 7)

The Census Bureau and the CDC face similar problems and have similar mechanisms in place to minimize them. The CDC has two broad sources of information. One, it assembles data gathered by hospitals (e.g., injuries and illness), state departments (birth, deaths, marriages, etc.), public health agencies (vaccinations), nursing homes, and individual physicians. Two, it also conducts some of its own interviews and physical exams at remote centers (2016). This two-prong approach can be quite revealing when determining the frequency of gunshot homicides, assaults, suicides, and accidents.

Data from all these government sources are also often used in case control studies. Researchers conducting these studies may supplement government data with some they collect on their own; for instance, they may interview and track people treated for gunshot injuries in the local emergency room.

Finally, the government data is a common source of information used by individual researchers, whether they be advocates of a serious right to bear arms or serious gun control. They mine these large data sets seeking to isolate relevant factors and to identify causal relationships. Different researchers manipulate, analyze, and interpret this data differently.

DATA COLLECTED BY INSTITUTES AND INSTITUTIONS

Sometimes data is collected by academic institutions like the Harvard Injury Control Research Center and the General Sciences Survey, overseen by the National Science Research Center at the University of Chicago. Usually these data sets are larger than those collected by individual researchers and smaller than those collected by government agencies. However, the sets are often substantial; and these institutions have a long history of doing high-quality, highly respected research. Hence, on some issues, these may provide invaluable data.

DATA COLLECTED BY INDIVIDUAL RESEARCHERS OR TEAMS

The limitations of some current data sources prompted some researchers to gather their own data. We should not categorically dismiss these efforts. We should not assume that large-scale data is always more reliable. An individual or a team may be meticulous. She (or it) may provide a novel way of gathering, interpreting, and assessing current data. Her analysis may be insightful. Generally, we will find such research more convincing if it is consistent with, manages to fill worrisome gaps in, or provides plausible explanations for large-scale data. Conversely, if studies based on such data clash with findings in larger scale studies, then the researchers should explain why their research is more reliable despite its limitations. They may meet that burden. However, it is a burden not easily meet. Especially for surveys.

DATA BASED ON SURVEYS

Surveys face multiple obstacles. One, as I noted earlier, the subject class may not represent the target class. Even if the subject class is representative, if the researchers get a low response rate (i.e., a very large percentage of people asked to participate refuse), that will likely skew their results (Wellford, C. F. et al. 2004: 37). Two, the information researchers collect from the subjects may be incomplete, inaccurate, or improperly classified. Researchers must ensure that they ask enough—but not too many—questions, and they must phrase the questions in ways more likely to elicit informative and precise answers. That is easier said than done. I am careful to precisely word paper and exam topics so I can determine students' knowledge of the issues and their ability to think critically about them. However, far more often than I dare admit, I later noticed that my wording was imprecise or ambiguous. Surveys are at least as subject to unclarity or ambiguity. After all, the students in my classes have related to me for the entire semester and so are more likely to construe my questions in the ways I intended. In contrast, a randomly selected group of people from different educational, social, economic, and cultural backgrounds will be unacquainted with the researcher and therefore more likely to misunderstand or misinterpret even a seemingly precisely worded question. Consequently, the subjects' answers may lead researchers to draw inappropriate inferences.

Third, we have substantial evidence of the power of "framing effects" to shape how people interpret questions (Sinnott-Armstrong, W. 2008: 815-821). Their wording and context (e.g., the order in which they are asked) shapes the listener's understanding, and therefore, influences how they answer the questions. Experimenters may thereby elicit misleading answers.

Fourth, if researchers ask subjects about their observations, they must remember that the weakness of eyewitness testimony is "an established body of knowledge" (American Psychological Association 2011: 14). This gives us some reason to doubt reported observations of even careful subjects. It is not only that people incorrectly report what they saw, heard, smelled, or felt, they may also draw flawed inferences from their experiences, especially if they are reporting a highly stressful encounter. Thus, some could mistakenly interpret an innocent but peculiar individual as an aggressor. She might assume that someone has a gun, when that person does not. She could also conclude that another person was frightened off by the sight of her gun, while other explanations (a barking dog in the background) are as, if not more, plausible.

Fifth, there are other ways the subjects can misinterpret experience by misjudging what caused what. If a robber knew that someone in a house had a gun, then we would have some reason to think that he was thereby deterred from robbing that house. I am confident this sometimes happens. However, if I have a gun and no one robs me, it would be premature to infer that the gun deterred potential robbers.

None of this is to say that we cannot obtain relevant empirical data that might guide our thinking on these policy issues. What it does say is that surveys can go wrong in many ways. We must be acutely aware of these scientific potholes when creating and conducting studies.

ISSUES COMPLICATING THE EVALUATION
OF ALL RESEARCH

Lurking in the background of all these discussions is that the design, execution, and interpretation of all three types of studies relies on informed armchair arguments. Gary Kleck would disagree. He claims armchair arguments are usually useless and often grotesquely misleading. In his words, "it is just as easy to build speculative critiques against good research as against bad" (Kleck, G. 1997/2006: 37). Given his examples of "speculative critiques," I assume he thinks armchair arguments are speculative critiques. By "speculative" he clearly means something akin to "pure fiction." However, in suggesting that all armchair arguments are fictions, he errs. As I argued in chapter 2, we can neither design nor evaluate studies without *informed* armchair arguments.

The need for such knowledge is especially high when designing, conducting, and evaluating surveys. We must use informed background information when deciding how to identify subjects and how to classify their answers. The divergence in individuals' answers to survey questions will be more common and substantial than are the responses of police who interpret their information using the FBI Handbook's guidelines.

With this general information in hand, I will, in the following chapter, summarize the proffered empirical evidence. In chapter 7, I evaluate this purported evidence.

Chapter 6

The Empirical Evidence

In this chapter I summarize the empirical evidence advocates offer in favor and against forms of gun control. In the next chapter I assess those arguments. These arguments play two distinctive albeit overlapping roles in the gun control debate. One, they are used expressly to support or criticize claims about the costs or benefits of widespread private gun ownership. Two, since the strongest arguments for a right to bear arms construe guns as an effective or necessary or reasonable means to one's self-defense, then empirical evidence can support or undermine claims about the existence and strength of an instrumental right to bear arms.

THE BENEFITS OF GUNS

Gun advocates' principal empirical claim is that guns are highly beneficial to law-abiding owners and to society at large, while any costs of extensive private gun ownership are relatively minor. Most arguments focus on using firearms for private self-defense, although, there is a related argument I mentioned, and briefly discuss here and more extensively in the next chapter.

I focus on the work of Gary Kleck and John Lott, Jr., since these researchers have generated the most extensive literature and are most frequently cited by gun advocates. Each is responsible for one of the two pillars of most pro-gun arguments.

Gary Kleck: Defensive Gun Uses Are Common and Effective

Kleck's entry into the gun control debate began with the publication of *Point Blank: Guns and Violence in America* (1991). In that book he claimed there were many more defensive gun uses (DGUs) than most people supposed. Kleck moved to the forefront of the debate, when, four years later, he published a coauthored essay that upwardly revised DGU estimates (Kleck, G. and Gertz, M. 1995).

He and Gertz claimed they needed to conduct their study since all previous ones were flawed. The principal target of their criticism was the National Crime Victimization Survey (NCVS). Conducted semi-annually by the US Census Bureau, the NCVS bases its findings on reports from interviews with 90,000 households. The NCVS has consistently found fewer than 100,000 DGUs annually, usually around 70,000 (Bureau of Justice Statistics 2017). In contrast, the thirteen studies cited by Kleck and Gertz found a much higher number of DGUs, although only two had numbers as high as theirs.

Kleck and Gertz offer five reasons for thinking that the NCVS is deeply flawed. One, it is inconsistent with findings in the thirteen aforementioned studies (1995: 153). They find this consideration so decisive that they are shocked that the Bureau of Justice Statistics disseminates the NCVS's findings. Clearly they assume these other studies are not just different but demonstrably and uncontroversially superior. Second, the NCVS findings are suspect since the interviews were not anonymous. This increases the chance that many respondents will give dishonest answers. Third, the interviewees knew that the interviewers worked at least temporarily for the government. This would make many interviewees reluctant to admit a self-defensive gun use since they might fear that by having or using a gun they have acted illegally.

Fourth, the interviewees "are never directly asked whether they used a gun for self-protection. They are asked only general questions about whether they did anything to protect themselves" (1995: 155). I infer that Kleck and Gertz think a survey can effectively study DGUs only if that is the study's express purpose and if the researchers announce that purpose at the beginning of each interview. I assume they think that otherwise a significant number of respondents will offer false or incomplete responses. Fifth, the person interviewed spoke for everyone in the household.

These five factors show that the NCVS is "singularly ill-suited to the task of estimating DGU frequency" (1995: 154). Among other things, it explains why 97% of people who had used a gun in self-defense would not offer accurate DGU information to NCVS interviewers. I think most people can imagine why at least some of these factors could explain some underreporting. The authors did not explain how these led to such massive underreporting.

They claim the NCVS's failures stem from the fact that it "was not designed to estimate how often people resist crime using a gun. It was designed primarily to estimate national victimization levels; it incidentally includes a few self-protection questions which include response categories covering resistance with a gun" (Kleck, G. and Gertz, M. 1995: 156).

Although they deem the original thirteen studies superior to the NCVS, they note that most of these surveys were also not expressly about defensive gun use. Despite their purported superiority to the NCVS, "none of them are very thorough or satisfactory for estimating DGU frequency, even though they otherwise seem to have been conducted quite professionally" (1995: 157). Additionally, most of these studies, like the NCVS, asked the interviewees to report not only their own DGU use but also that of anyone in the household

(1995: 157). Finally, some of these surveys asked about DGUs over a person's lifetime; some did not exclude use of guns against animals, and so on. These—and other—weaknesses are precisely why Kleck and Gertz designed and conducted their own survey. If the thirteen studies were adequate, they did not need to do another one. What I find intriguing is that the authors do not explain why they think these studies are superior to the NCVS, especially since all have one or more inadequacies they consider decisive marks against the NCVS.

Before proceeding to describe Kleck and Gertz's survey, the reader should note that all of these objections, with the *possible* exception of the first, are armchair arguments. You may recall that in chapter 2, I claimed that armchair arguments are critical for both designing and evaluating empirical arguments. By their words, Kleck and Gertz reinforce that claim. They use background knowledge to explain why they think the NCVS survey is flawed and why the standard interpretations of its findings are indefensible. This—like the discussion of Stell's argument in the previous chapter—shows that and why there is no sensible way to resolve this debate with bare empirical data. We cannot conduct well-designed studies or interpret their purported findings without informed armchair arguments.

KLECK AND GERTZ'S SURVEY

Kleck and Gertz's survey is the first "ever [expressly] devoted to the subject of armed defense." They successfully interviewed nearly 5,000 people, 61% of those they tried to contact. They oversampled in the South and the West and in households with males since these respondents were "more likely to own [a] gun and to be victims of crimes in which victims might use guns defensively. Data were later weighted to adjust for oversampling" (1995: 161). They did not fully explain why they oversampled and then adjusted for such oversampling. I presume they thought it would result in more accurate findings.

They claimed that theirs was "the most anonymous possible national survey. . . . We did not know the identities of those who were interviewed, and made this fact clear to the Rs" (1995: 160). The interviewers asked whoever answered the phone about their own and other household residents' defensive gun use. Initially, Rs (respondents) were asked about any such experiences in the past five years; depending on their answer, they were then asked about any such experiences in the past year. Once the interviewees claimed they had used a gun defensively, "we asked a long series of detailed questions designed to establish exactly what Rs did with their guns; for example, if they had confronted other humans, and how had each DGU connected to a specific crime or crimes" (1995: 160). Finally, to ensure that the initial interviewers correctly reported what the respondents told them, "all interviews in which an alleged DGU was reported by the R were validated by supervisors with call-backs" (1995: 161). Finally, the authors state they used only the most reliable reports and interpreted the data conservatively. They did not explain exactly what either of these methodological constraints required and how it ensured the accuracy of their reported findings.

Of the completed interviews, 222 people reported a DGU at some point during the past five years. When they reported multiple DGUs, they were asked detailed questions about the most recent event. Using the percentage of interviewees who claimed they used a gun defensively, Kleck and Gertz inferred that there were between 2.2 to 2.5 million DGUs per year. These estimates are twenty-five times higher than those of the NCVS and higher than most of the other studies they cite approvingly. Nonetheless, they contend their estimates were more accurate since their study was superior in three ways: "(1) a shorter recall period; (2) reliance on person-based information rather than just household-based information; and

(3) information on how many household DGUs had been experienced in the recall period by those Rs reporting any such experiences" (1995: 165).

There were several facts about Kleck's survey and findings I note because they inform my evaluation of his argument in the following chapter. First, 85% of the reports of DGUs came from the person originally interviewed (I assume the person answering the phone) (1995: 165). This is very odd. Second, nearly one-third of those who reported a DGU reported they had more than one DGU in the past five years, with an average of 1.5 DGUs (1995: 166).

Third, a stated implication of the survey's findings is that 97% of the people the NCVS interviewed who had had a DGU did not report that encounter to the NCVS interviewer. Four, although the NCVS is not good at reporting DGUs, Kleck and Gertz think it is a fine instrument for reporting *criminal* gun use. That survey found that there were slightly more than half a million criminal gun uses each year. By combining this figure from the NCVS with their study's estimates of the number of DGUs, Kleck and Gertz infer that annually there are more than four times as many *defensive* gun uses than *offensive* gun uses (1995: 170).

Five, the survey that shows that there are 2.5 million DGUs annually also finds that defensive guns users have "certainly or almost certainly saved" 400,000 lives annually (Kleck, G. 1997/2006: 174).

KLECK'S ELABORATION

Two years after publishing the essay with Gertz, Kleck published his second book on the topic, *Targeting Guns: Firearms and Their Control* (1997/2006). In it he reiterates and amplifies findings in his previous work, criticizes the work of many supporting gun control, and responds to some criticisms of his earlier work. Taken as a whole, the book is a mixture of empirical and armchair reasoning. He cites numerous studies, most commonly his own. He often wields armchair objections against others' views and uses them to rebut their objections to his research. This is normal.

He devotes considerable space criticizing others. In itself, this is not surprising. What is surprising is that he does not often offer arguments explaining where and why their views are misleading or inaccurate. Instead, he pans their knowledge or their research skills. He takes special aim at those publishing in medical journals. Most of their work, he says, is

> technically primitive, relying on research methods that most so-
> cial scientists would regard as reflective of the technical standards
> of the mid-1960s or earlier. More specifically, the research com-
> monly (1) uses simple univariate or bi-variate analyses rather
> than multi-variate procedures that control for variables that may
> confound the relationship between violence and guns or gun
> control, (2) ignores the possible two-way relationship between
> guns and violence . . . (3) uses primitive invalid measures of gun
> availability (or none at all), (4) relies on small local samples that
> are not representative of any larger population. (1997/2006: 32)

These researchers are also pervasively biased. "Among ideologues involved in research, the common practice is to do just enough research to support the conclusions they personally favor on emotional grounds" (1997/2006: 33). Moreover, these pro-control advocates engage in "selective omission" of studies they do not like (1997/2006: 38-39). Put more bluntly, he avers that many of them are dishonest. "There has probably been more outright dishonesty in addressing the issue of the frequency of DGU than any other issue in the gun-control debate" (1997/2006: 154).

Although this criticism of others takes center stage in the early chapters of the book, it is not the book's primary focus. Its core aim is to defend his earlier finding that there are at least 2.5 million annual

DGUs in the United States. This is Kleck's most significant claim, which, if true, would give considerable weight to the assertion that allowing citizens to own guns is vital for their self-defense. He also discusses a number of related themes about the use of guns. A few of these I briefly discuss shortly. Most are either criticisms of specific claims in favor of gun control or rebuttals of criticisms of his views. I develop and evaluate those in the following chapter.

Kleck devotes most of one chapter, and elements of others, discussing policies to control specific firearms: for example, handguns and assault weapons. He argues that banning Saturday night specials and assault weapons, as well as accessories like "cop killer" ammo, will not save many lives since few people are killed by criminals wielding these weapons. In the one case where a ban (all handguns) might save some lives, the benefit would come at an enormous cost: it would (a) deprive law-abiding citizens of weapons they need to defend themselves and (b) prompt criminals to use more lethal weapons, for instance, long guns (1997/2006: 136–139) since they will have more difficulty obtaining handguns.

He also categorically rejects the suggestion that it is generally better for victims not to resist criminals. He states that potential victims who resist, and especially those who resist with a gun, are less likely to be killed, injured, or have their property stolen than are those who resist using any other means (knife, blunt object, or fists) or do not resist at all.

How does the private ownership of guns have so many positive benefits? He thinks it stems fairly straightforwardly from most criminals' motivation. Out of a concern for self-preservation, criminals are less likely to attack individuals they think might have a gun (1997/2006: 248; he expresses a similar view on pp. 149, 170, 180, 192 and elsewhere). At least they are deterred from attacking people by themselves and without being heavily armed. They choose how to act based on their judgments of the likely outcomes of their actions. Finally, he contends that although gun-toting robbers are more likely to *intend* to harm their victims (1997/2006: 230), they are less likely to actually harm their victims since the gun serves "as a substitute for actual attack" (1997/2006: 225).

John Lott, Jr.: The Benefits of Permitting Citizens to Carry Arms in Public

Lott provides the second pillar of most common pro-gun arguments. While Kleck emphasizes broad benefits of having an armed citizenry, Lott focuses almost exclusively on the benefits of right-to-carry laws in the United States. His initial work analyzed data from 1977 to 1992 (Lott, J. R., Jr. and Mustard, D. B. 1997); the ideas and methodology from that study were expanded in his *More Guns, Less Crime*. In the second edition of the book, he analyzed four more years of data; in the third edition, he examined nine additional years (2010/2000/1997). I rely primarily on his final rendering of the methodology described in the 2010 version of that book.

He consistently found that shall-issues laws—laws *requiring* authorities to issue carry permits to all but a small number of people (former felons and the mentally ill)—reduces violent crime without significantly increasing accidental deaths. The declines in violent crime occur almost immediately after passage of the law, continue over time, especially as the number of permits increase. The findings reveal that "for every 1,000 additional people with permits, there are 0.3 fewer murders, 2.4 fewer rapes, 21 fewer robberies, and 14.1 fewer aggravated assaults" (2010/2000/1997: 3013).

Lott and Mustard's plan was to identify cross-sectional, time series data from each county to determine "whether the crime rates change [in shall-issue states] relative to other changes in counties located in states without such laws" (Lott, J. R., Jr. 2010/2000/1997). It is cross-sectional in that it compares counties to counties; it is time series inasmuch as it compares the data over time—before, during, and after passage of the shall-issue laws. The third edition continues this comparison by looking at twenty-one additional states that adopted such laws from 1993 to 2007 (2010/2000/1997: 1025).

Lott concluded:

> When state concealed-handgun laws went into effect in a county, murders fell by about 8 percent, rapes fell by 5 percent, and aggravated assaults fell by 7 percent.... The estimated coefficients suggest that if... [all other jurisdictions] had... been forced to issue handgun permits, murders in the United States would have declined by about 1,400. (2010/2000/1997: 1136)

He chose to measure county figures, rather than state ones, since "both crime and arrest rates vary widely within states.... [T]he variation in both crime rates and arrest rates across states is almost always smaller than the average within-state variation across counties" (2010/2000/1997: 788).

To ensure that the study did not overlook some relevant factors that might explain the measured effects, he controlled for arrest rates and thirty-sex demographic categories—race, gender, age, and whether people lived in an urban or rural area, among others (2010/2000/1997: 2778, 5781). The result, he claims, is the most thorough and comprehensive study ever conducted on the topic.

He uses this data not only to support shall-issue carry laws but also to criticize establishing and maintaining gun-free zones. Gun-free zones are locales where guns are typically not permitted: most schools, government buildings, hospitals, and bars. Lott considers these laws the height of stupidity. It is an open invitation to mass murder (2010/2000/1997: 5418).

Common Themes

Despite their differences in emphases, both advocates share several beliefs.

1. Guns are effective means of defense. By using them, people may stop an assault in progress or at least diminish its harm.
2. Efforts to control guns deny law-abiding citizens an effective means of self-defense.
3. Criminals are rational: they alter their behavior based on their assessment of likely consequences of available actions. Many criminals will be less likely to attack someone they fear or think or know has a gun. These criminals will either commit fewer crimes or they will seek less dangerous targets, for instance, unoccupied homes or people they are confident do not have firearms.
4. Laws that seriously limit access to handguns will encourage criminals to have, carry, and use more lethal weapons (shotguns, rifles, etc.).

In sum, each thinks that widespread private ownership of guns is highly beneficial. Any costs of private ownership pale in comparison to its benefits. This is precisely what those who advocate stricter gun control deny.

THE COST OF GUNS

Those who favor serious gun control want fewer guns available to fewer people and more restrictions on the ones that private citizens can own. They think the benefits of private gun ownership, although real, are less extensive than supporters claim, and that the costs are far greater than gun supporters acknowledge. Intelligent gun control can lower the costs of gun ownership without substantially lowering its benefits.

The most prominent academic spokespeople for serious gun control are physicians and public health professionals. The purpose of the "prohealth" approach is to institute regulatory interventions that will lessen the number of deaths and injuries caused by firearms. Society should protect citizens not only from intentional wrongdoing but also from harm caused by everyday human error. David Hemenway muses that as a youngster he began "to realize that [some of] my schoolmates would probably still be alive if the cars in which they were riding were more forgiving of human error and bad judgment" (2010/2006: 92).

Caring governments should work to reduce all harms, including firearm harm: "both intentional and unintentional shootings, both self-inflicted and inflicted by others. . . . These policies would do little to affect the limited safety benefits derived from firearms but would substantially reduce the major health and human problems" (2010/2006: 118, 125).

This prohealth approach has been very successful in multiple venues. It reduced deaths of and injuries to people in widely different environments: workers (OSHA); people living in their homes (requiring GFCI plugs in bathrooms and kitchens); drivers (requiring them to use seat belts, new cars to have airbags); and children sleeping in their cribs, playing with their toys, or romping on local playgrounds. We can see these benefits fairly dramatically if we compare accidental deaths in highly regulated New York state to that of the rest of the nation. New York has nearly 40% fewer accidental injury deaths than the national average (Kegler, S. R. et al. 2017). These public health researchers contend that this orientation can help us isolate ways to save lives and diminish harms that occur when many people own firearms.

Following are the obvious and not-so-obvious costs of permitting most people to have relatively unrestricted access to firearms.

Homicides

Public health researchers recognize that there are plausible armchair reasons for thinking that high gun prevalence in an area will stop some crimes in progress and will deter some contemplating committing crimes. At the same time, there are also plausible armchair reasons for thinking that high gun prevalence will increase violent crime, including homicides.

Some researchers use case control studies to determine if there is a causal connection between private gun ownership and homicides. Often they do multiple studies within a single city. There are three studies of Detroit homicides, conducted from the early 1950s to the early 1990s. Each found "a positive and statistically significant association between gun density and homicide" (Hepburn, L. M. and Hemenway, D. 2004: 430).

Researchers also conduct large-scale epidemiological studies. Some compare ownership and homicide rates between cities; others, between states; and still others, between different regions of the United States. Finally, some compare ownership and homicide rates in the United States to rates in other developed countries.

All these studies suggest that high private gun ownership increases homicides. At the state level, researchers found "a positive and significant association between gun ownership and homicide rates for the entire population and for every age group (except 1–4)" (Miller, M., Azrael, D., and Hemenway D. 2002b: 434–435). The correlation was quite high when comparing states with the highest levels of gun ownership to those with the lowest (Miller, M. et al. 2002b: 435). At the regional level, they found a similar, but not quite statistically significant, association.

Researchers aver that international evidence is even more compelling. They find a high correlation between private gun prevalence and both gun homicide rates and overall homicide rates. This highlights a feature of their arguments that requires some explanation: sometimes public health researchers look specifically at *gun* homicide rates. One might wonder why. There is a plausible rationale. Unless we think there is a *complete* substitution effect—that every murder committed with a firearm would have been committed in some other way were firearms not readily available—then lowering the gun homicide rate *will* lower the overall homicide rate. Of course, most people acknowledge that there is *some* substitution effect; at the same time, few people think there is a *complete* substitution effect. Some studies find almost no substitution effect. Several found that lowering gun homicide rates actually lowers the non-gun homicide rate (Miller, M., Azrael, D., and Hemenway D. 2002a).

Unfortunately, inferring a causal connection between two correlated factors is iffy since, as these pro-control researchers recognize, the relationships between these two factors can be bidirectional.

> [H]igh levels of firearm availability might lead to higher homicide rates, and higher homicide rates may lead to more people acquiring firearms. . . . [F]irearm regulations can directly affect both gun availability and homicide rates, and both firearm ownership levels and homicide rates may influence whether or not firearm regulations are enacted. (Miller M. et al. 2002a)

Even if we are unsure of the causal relation, one fact should give pro-gun advocates extreme pause: the "nongun homicide rate [in the United States] is higher than the total homicide rates of almost all other high-income nations" (Hemenway, D. 2010/2006: 1246). That is something that calls for explanation. The public health researchers think that the best explanation is that high private ownership of guns increases people's propensity to commit homicide. Of course, one might simply conclude that Americans are simply an especially violent people. Although one might make that inference, it is not an especially flattering or satisfying retort. Moreover, were it true, then public health researchers would have one more reason for thinking that making more guns available to more people in more ways and places would only increase violence in a society that is already violence prone.

Suicides

Most Americans who died from gunshots committed suicide. The majority of suicides for all ages are committed with a firearm; 50% more than by all other means combined (Centers for Disease Control and Prevention 1997: table 7). We know suicide is a problem; we know guns play an unusually prominent role in American suicides. What we have trouble determining is whether gun prevalence *causes* suicides. How could that be established? Case control studies are the easiest to conduct. Unfortunately, as I noted in the previous chapter, these studies usually involve small numbers of subjects. That makes their findings less compelling.

Still, control advocates claim that the case studies we do have are highly suggestive. One of them examined 353 suicides. The authors found, "The association between handgun purchase and suicide tended to become stronger as the number of handguns purchased increased" [the association was statistically significant] (Miller, M. and Hemenway, D. 1999: 65). More specifically, "all case-control studies indicate that a gun in the home is significantly associated with a higher risk of suicide, *especially among youth*" (Miller, M. and Hemenway, D. 1999: 73; emphasis mine).

One long-term epidemiological study reinforces these case control findings. Researchers looked at the patterns of guns ownership over thirty years to determine whether there had been a parallel change in both firearm prevalence and total suicides. The findings were evocative both in the population as a whole and within each of the four census regions. The association was most dramatic for people under the age nineteen. "The magnitude of the association between changes in household firearm prevalence and rates of firearm and overall suicide was greatest for children: for each 10% decline in the percentage of households containing both children and firearms, the rate of firearm suicide among children 0–19 years of age dropped 8.3% . . . and the rate of overall suicide dropped 4.1%" (Centers for Disease Control and Prevention 2016; Miller, M. and Hemenway, D. 2008; see alsoTavernise, S. 2016).

This later finding is especially relevant when debating gun control. For although the total suicide rate is arguably a morally relevant consideration, as I explained in chapter 2, children committing suicide is indisputably relevant. Children lack the intellectual, volitional, and emotional skills, as well as the fortitude, to make such a momentous choice.

Public health researchers claim that gun prevalence is highly correlated with the rate of children's suicide. In 1997, the CDC found that the suicide rate among US teenagers was twice that of twenty-six other industrialized countries, primarily because the *gun* suicide rate among this age group was fifteen times the average for those other countries. Independent researchers found similar results decades later (Grinshteyn, E. and Hemenway, D. 2016). Public health officials contend this finding provides strong reason to limit children's access to firearms (LaFollette, H. 2001).

Accidental Deaths

Relatively few people are killed in gun accidents annually. However, researchers claim that we get a better sense of the magnitude of the problem if we think about it over time compared to other causes of death during the same period.

Between 1965 and 2000, more than sixty thousand Americans died from unintentional firearm shootings. That is more Americans than were killed in our wars or from coal mine injuries during the same period. In the 1990s, an average of twelve hundred Americans died each year from gun "accidents." (Hemenway, D. 2010/2006: 626–628)

Kleck downplays the significance of these numbers. He claims that people who die in gun accidents tend to be criminals or at least antisocial. Hemenway offers empirical and moral objections to this argument. First, he says that the claim is false: there is no evidence that accident victims are especially antisocial. Second—and more directly critical of Kleck's moral stance—Hemenway avers that even if Kleck were correct, that fact would be morally irrelevant.

Even if 100 percent of the shooters had been involved in previous violent incidents or motor vehicle collisions, should that mitigate our efforts to prevent them from accidentally shooting themselves and others? Drivers involved in motor vehicle collisions are more likely than other motorists to have alcohol problems, traffic violations, and arrests for violence.... These facts have not prevented rational policy from [seeking and] achieving a dramatic reduction in motor vehicle injuries. (2010/2006: 544–547)

Serious Injuries

Not everyone who is shot dies. At least 70% of gunshot victims are not killed (Kleck, G. 1997/2006: 266). Although some people's injuries are minor, the number with serious gunshot injuries is substantial. In 2011 more than 30,000 gunshot victims required hospitalization (they were not just treated and released) (Fields, G. and McWhirter, C. 2012). This occurred during a time when insurance companies, in an effort to contain costs, encouraged hospitals to release patients as quickly as feasible. Therefore, we can infer that if hospitals had followed previous standard practices, then even more gunshot victims would have been hospitalized.

Of those with serious injuries, some suffer traumatic brain or spinal cord injuries, and more than half still have clinical symptoms of PTSD three years after the incident (Hemenway, D. 2010/ 2006: 203–205). One way of seeing the size and severity of the problem is to note that gun shots are *the* leading cause of uninsured hospital stays in the United States (Hemenway, D. 2010/2006: 211). We must consider these consequences when counting the relative costs and benefits of people privately owning guns.

Broader Costs of Gun Violence

The costs of the private ownership of guns are not only the obvious ones we have been discussing. There are also the medical costs; lost work days, months, or years; and lost spending power. Moreover, these physical and economic costs do not exhaust the serious consequences. We must also consider wider social and personal costs.

> Most all of us bear some part of the costs of gun violence, in myriad ways: waiting in line to pass through airport security; buying a transparent book bag for school aged children to meet their school's post-Columbine regulations; paying taxes for the protection of public officials, for urban renewal projects in areas devastated by gun violence, for subsidizing an urban trauma center; living in fear that one's children may be injured by a stray bullet or that a despondent relative would get her hands on a

gun. And no one is entirely safe from becoming a victim them-selves. (Cook, P. J. and Ludwig, J. 2002: 28)

There are other more diffuse ancillary costs. One way of seeing how significant these can be is to remember how the fear of polio put many people in this country on edge, and how its eventual eradication benefited everyone.

The savings to society from this miracle include the costs avoided from acute and long-term medical care of victims, the suffering of victims and their families, and the lost productivity of those who died young or were permanently disabled. But the savings were not limited to the costs associated with suffering the disease; also important was the elimination of any need for families and public agencies to take precautions, or even to worry about the possibility of someone they cared about being stricken. (Cook, P. J. and Ludwig, J. 2002: 522)

We would also see similar benefits if we could find effective ways of lessening gun violence There will be fewer victims, less stress and fear, "a reduced homicide caseload in the criminal justice system, in a revival of [previously] violence-impacted neighborhoods, [and] in the emotional relief to mothers now concerned about their children's safety" (Cook, P. J. and Ludwig, J. 2002: 541).

THE EVIDENCE IS UNCLEAR

Those who support the private ownership of guns are certain of the guns' benefits; those who support more extensive gun control are confident of guns' costs. Others claim that although the available evidence may be suggestive, it is neither compelling nor univocal.

The National Research Council's Committee to Improve Research Information and Data on Firearms concluded at the end of its 2005 study that empirical research on firearms and violence has resulted in important findings. . . . [We have] a wealth of descriptive information about the prevalence of firearm-related injuries and deaths, about firearms markets, and about the relationships between rates of gun ownership and violence. . . . [At the same time, we have a] relative absence of credible data central to addressing even the most basic questions about firearms and violence. . . . [W]ithout much better data, important questions will continue to be unanswerable. (Wellford, C. F., Pepper, J. V. and Petrie, C. V. 2004: 2)

The empirical problems are not confined to one side of this debate. The committee found no "credible evidence that the passage of right-to-carry laws decreases or increases violent crime, and there is almost no empirical evidence that the . . . prevention programs focused on gun-related violence have had any effect on children's behavior, knowledge, attitudes, or beliefs about firearms" (Wellford, C. F. et al. 2004: 2).

The difficulties the research study group cited are not unique to gun research; they are "common to all social science research." Drawing reasonable causal inferences is always complicated. The methods used are sometimes questionable; the data acquired is often thin. We don't know enough about the "adverse outcomes associated with firearms," and we don't have enough evidence on the existing ownership of guns (Wellford, C. F. et al. 2004: 3). We need a national data-collection system akin to the pilot collection program like that established by the Harvard School of Public Health's Injury Control Research Center (Wellford, C. F. et al. 2004: 3).

Having acknowledged the overall inadequacy of gun research, the National committee singled out Kleck's and Lott's claims for explicit criticism. They offer an extended discussion of the purported benefits of right-to-carry laws offered by Lott:

> It is not possible to reach any scientifically supported conclusion becauseof (a) the sensitivity of the empirical results to seemingly minor changes in model specification, (b) a lack of robustness of the results to the inclusion of more recent years of data (during which there were many more law changes than in the earlier period), and (c) the statistical imprecision of the results. The evidence to date does not adequately indicate either the sign or the magnitude of a causal link between the passage of right-to-carry laws and crime rates. (Wellford, C. F. et al. 2004: 7)

One member of the study group rejects the larger group's conclusion: he thought Lott's studies were compelling. The committee emphatically repudiated this dissenter's claim and rationale. We "find his [the author's] arguments to be unconvincing and his summary of some parts of the chapter inaccurate" (Wellford, C. F. et al. 2004: 274). A second member also wrote a partial dissent. He thinks the committee was unduly optimistic about the ability to resolve these issues experimentally (Horowitz, J. L. 2004: 299). I explore his arguments in the following chapter.

CONCLUSION

We find ourselves with three divergent claims: one, several individuals—Kleck and Lott in particular—extol the enormous benefits of the private ownership of guns. Two, most public health and medical researchers downplay their benefits and focus instead on the significant costs of private gun ownership—costs pro-gun people deny. Three, a National Research Council's Committee concluded that (a) claims about the number of Defensive Gun Uses are unsubstantiated (Wellford, C. F. et al. 2004: 114), rejected (b) assertions about the enormous benefits of shall-issue carry permits, and, finally, concluded (c) the research on the connections between guns and homicide, violent crimes in general, suicide, and accidents are less than convincing.

In the face of such disagreement, what is an honest, curious citizen or legislator supposed to do?

Chapter 7

Evaluating the Empirical Evidence

Most readers will find the previous chapter unsettling. It was unsettling to write. It is unnerving and confusing to find putative authorities advancing incompatible empirical claims. After all, most people are inclined to think that empirical claims are demonstrable and not standardly in dispute.

However, those familiar with the nature of science understand that this latter supposition is a modern fairy tale. Science thrives on disagreements and anomalies (findings that do not match theoretical expectations). Scientific glitches and uncertainties drive discovery, prompt scientists to reexamine their beliefs to ensure that what they think is true, *is* true. If they discover that received science is mistaken, then they can right the ship of science.

Unfortunately, in our world what drives many so-called scientific doubts is not scientific uncertainty but ignorant or concocted "doubt." Even when the evidence is overwhelming, some people are unwilling to abandon a pet view, particularly if it has religious, personal, or financial ramifications she finds disquieting. Although the evidence in favor of the heliocentric view of the universe was overwhelming, it took two centuries before most people accepted it. These days, significant portions of Americans reject evolution because they, like their sixteenth-century precursors, think the theory clashes with their religious worldview. It does not matter that the evidence is clear and emphatic; it does not matter that most theologians do not think evolution conflicts with theism. It does not matter that the practice of modern medicine depends on the truth of the theory of evolution. They reject evolution because someone told them it was incompatible with their religious views.

People driven by pecuniary interests can also create faux doubt. It took decades for most people to overcome doubt fabricated to mask the vast evidence that cigarette smoking (and asbestos) caused cancer. More recently, some deny that climate change is occurring; others admit that it is happening while rejecting the scientifically accepted view that humans are largely to blame. Business interests thought (with smoking) and think (with climate change) that acknowledging the truth of these facts would hit their pocketbooks. They are right. So these interests have used (and are using) their vast power to convince the public that what is not disputable is, in fact, disputed (Michaels, D. 2008; Oreskes, N. and Conway, E. M. 2010). My claim, here, is not that the scientific consensus is never wrong. It is sometimes mistaken. That is why scientists should (and usually do) treat objections seriously, that way they can correct erroneous conceptions. We can challenge the majority view. However, it is inappropriate to do so with nothing more than fear or by fabricating evidence that clashes with it.

That is not our problem here. Although there is not any serious scientific doubt about the effects of smoking or the reality of climate change, there is scientific disagreement about the frequency of defensive gun use; the benefits of shall-issue carry laws; and the relationship between gun prevalence and homicides, suicides, and accidents. We should not blithely dismiss advocates of any persuasion as "scientific kooks," even if we ultimately decide, after more careful analysis, that some claims are more plausible and some researchers are more reliable.

This creates a problem for conscientious citizens and legislators who must decide whether to support or oppose a gun policy (or virtually any proposed legislative policy). A responsible citizen or legislator wants to make the best decision, that is, one that promotes the best overall outcome while respecting people's rights. How, though, can citizens or legislators decide what *is* the most defensible policy when authorities disagree about what the evidence is and what it shows? How can we decide whom to believe and why to believe them?

Obviously, we should not believe everyone who claims to be an authority. We should be inclined to believe someone only if she really is an authority. That is why an informed citizen or legislator must be able to recognize genuine expertise and then should be capable of understanding and evaluating the putative authority's claims. If the citizen or legislator were herself an authority on the issue, then although she might not have actually gathered empirical evidence herself, she would have the knowledge and skills to evaluate other authorities' claims. On this issue, at least, she would not have to defer to anyone's testimony. Conversely, if she is entirely ignorant of the issue—if she lacks the background knowledge to even vaguely understand the dispute, let alone evaluate it, and she is devoid of the relevant knowledge and skills, then she is forced to rely *entirely* on the (purported) authorities' claims. The problem is that if she is *wholly* ignorant of the issues, then it is difficult to know how she might distinguish genuine from faux authorities.

Luckily most of us are in the vast epistemological middle between the extremes. To varying degrees, each of us must rely on authorities. To varying degrees, most of us can make some informed judgments about which people are the best authorities; we can partly understand and evaluate their studies, findings, and inferences from these findings. Unfortunately, although many of us are able to make these judgments, often we do not. More often than we dare admit, we are intellectually lazy. We are more ignorant than we want to believe; we are sometimes embarrassingly close to being wholly ignorant. The tendency to overestimate our abilities is a danger to which each of us should be acutely attuned. We should take steps to inoculate ourselves against such ignorance (Dunning, D. 2005; Mill, J. S. 1985/ 1885; LaFollette, H. 2017).

Since this conundrum goes far beyond the issue of gun control, it would be helpful to think generally about how a conscientious person should proceed whenever she must partly (or largely) rely on expert testimony to evaluate policies on nuclear power plants, banning the use of asbestos, or requiring motorcyclists to wear helmets. Of course, any list of considerations I offer will be incomplete; some considerations may be misstated; all are open to refinement. However, I think I can offer some sensible guidelines for conscientious people wanting to thoughtfully evaluate competing experts and their respective claims.

In order to assess claims of competing authorities, we must think about what it means to be and how one becomes an expert; we must think about how to judge whether a purported expert is acting *as an expert* when addressing the issue at hand. We must use that information to determine if self-described experts are pukka and which are most reliable. After developing these broad principles, I use them to evaluate competing authorities and competing claims about available gun policies.

THE CRITERIA

Is the Purported Authority a Genuine Authority on the Topic?

If we rely on the testimony of experts, they should be genuine authorities. Normally we think of an authority as someone (a) who has specialized knowledge and training in the requisite discipline, and (b) who is recognized as an authority by other members of that discipline or subdiscipline. That means, though, that we can determine if someone has the requisite training only if we know which discipline(s) provide practitioners the requisite knowledge and skills to evaluate the topic at hand. Most of those who write on gun control are criminologists, economists, public health professions, and physicians. Do all or some members of these disciplines have the requisite knowledge and skills?

I suspect some disciplines are more likely to be better equipped to investigate this issue. However, the differences are not so apparent or substantial that I completely dismiss any. I think all are able to contribute; many do illuminate the topic.

It is not enough that person be "an expert," she must be able to deploy her expertise *to the topic* being discussed. I have been talking as if we can assess expertise by focusing simply on her knowledge of relevant facts and best methods, as well as her reasoning skills. These are clearly critical elements of expertise. Someone with limited knowledge and mediocre skills is not reliable. However, knowledge and skills, no matter how robust, are insufficient. She also needs the requisite intellectual and moral dispositions or virtues. She must be curious: she must want to know the truth and doggedly pursue it. She must be intellectually honest: she must be willing to go where the arguments take her, even if it is not where she wants to go. She must be cautious: she should not make unduly grand claims about her expertise or about facts she has uncovered. She should not rashly judge other seeming experts. Finally, she must be trustworthy. The point is not simply that she should not lie. Indeed, I think it is best to assume that experts do not knowingly tell falsehoods. What is more important is that she should be unbiased; that is, she should not be so predisposed to reach a desired conclusion that she cannot honestly consider contrary evidence. An expert with all these dispositions is more likely to be open-minded, more willing to admit errors, shortcomings, and weak arguments. She is more likely to revise her views in light of new evidence.

Are We Capable of Evaluating Their Expertise?

Asking this question this way might imply that there are genuine experts; our job is simply to identify them and then believe whatever they say. The issue is more complicated. It is not enough to identify an expert and then straightway believe all her pronouncements. We must first decide if these advocates are sufficiently authoritative so that we should take their claims seriously. To do that, we must determine how to assess their degree of expertise and then examine the plausibility of their expert claims.

This is not an insurmountable problem since *very* few people completely lack the ability to distinguish an eminent expert from a charlatan. Those few who cannot will be unable to distinguish plausible authoritative claims from claptrap. They are at the mercy of the rhetorical powers of purported authorities and their running dogs.

Luckily most of us have some ability to identify experts; we can employ both direct and indirect means. In the Internet age, we can find and examine purported experts' credentials. We can thereby determine if they meet minimum requirements for relevant expertise; by looking at citation statistics we can usually ascertain their professional standing. We can also employ indirect means to ascertain their degree of expertise by observing how they professionally comport themselves. Do they exhibit the requisite knowledge, skills, and dispositions experts standardly have? Even if we cannot directly assess the putative expert's knowledge, usually we have some ability to identify her skills and dispositions.

There is no better place to begin than by using a basic expectation we have of genuine experts. We think that they should be able to explain (a) the methods they employ, (b) why they use them (and not others), (c) the results of their surveys or experiments, (d) the inferences they draw from the experiments' findings, and (e) how they are able to respond to criticisms others make of (a) through (d).

It is not just that they can explain each element; the best do so with aplomb. Stephen J. Gould, Carl Sagan, and more recently, Atul Gawande were/are exemplary thinkers, authors, and communicators. Reading anything written by them is a joy. Not everyone can write such sterling prose. Nonetheless, we see in them the importance of this skill. If a purported expert can provide a clear, sensible explanation for each element, I am more inclined to accept her authoritative announcements even when her detailed explanations are beyond my ken. Conversely, the murkier the purported expert's explanations, the less inclined I am to heed what she says, especially if I cannot directly assess her particular claims.

As you might imagine, if we are wholly incapable of judging *that someone is an expert,* we are unlikely to be able to evaluate her claims as an expert. Conversely, if we have the ability to determine that someone is an expert, we likely also have some ability to evaluate her studies. To judge the level of another's expertise and to assess her claims, we need (a) some awareness of how scientists design and execute studies (information of the sort summarized in chapter 5). We also (b) need sufficient reasoning skills to identify what we need to know to assess the implications of her assumptions and findings. Finally, we need (c) a modicum of the intellectual virtues experts need. With these in hand, we can judge an expert based on the clarity of her exposition and on the presence (or absence) of the other skills and dispositions mentioned above. Thus, we have some grounds for doubting her claims—or even her authority—if (1) she is insufficiently humble, (2) she is inconsistent, (3) she relies on dubious assumptions, (4) she makes questionable inferences or fails to see, acknowledge, and accept the implications of her premises, assumptions, or findings. Let me explain each of these before using them to evaluate the principal authors.

IS NOT APPROPRIATELY HUMBLE

Science advances when practitioners are open-minded and fallibalistic. They are more likely to spot and correct their own and other experts' judgments. However, one cannot be genuinely open-minded or fallibalistic if she is not appropriately humble. Being excessively boastful is not just unbecoming; such a person is less likely to be self-critical and intellectually honest and is more likely to succumb to the confirmatory bias (Nickerson, R. S. 1998; Kahneman, D. 2011: 81, 333). Such a purported expert is more likely to miss inconsistencies in her assumptions, inferences, or reasoning.

IS INCONSISTENT

Someone who is genuinely inconsistent (who claims both A and non-A) utters nonsense. Under these circumstances there is no way to discern what that person's view really is. In short, inconsistency is an intellectual guillotine; yet even the most careful person occasionally flirts with inconsistency, usually because we don't notice it; for instance, when our views are developed over an entire book written over many years (LaFollette, H. 2017). Moreover, we must remember that people's views evolve. While it might appear that a writer is inconsistent, it may simply show that she altered her views in light of new evidence.

Given how easy it is to be inconsistent, we can see why a purported expert needs to be scrupulously honest and self-critical. When the inconsistency is serious and pervasive, she undermines her status as an expert. It does not mean that everything she says is false; some of it may be spot on. Nonetheless it gives others reason to doubt her expert claims.

RELIES ON DUBIOUS EMPIRICAL
OR PSYCHOLOGICAL ASSUMPTIONS

As I mentioned in chapter 2, armchair arguments are essential for framing studies and evaluating results. We saw that phenomenon at play during the exposition in the previous chapter. Objections to adversaries' empirical studies are often armchair arguments based on background empirical evidence or psychological assumptions about what will or will not deter prospective criminals and about how they will respond if they think potential victims are armed or if handguns are no longer easily accessible. The more plausible these assumptions, the more telling the criticisms; the less plausible the assumptions, the less telling the criticisms. I will not say much about this consideration in the current chapter; I will, however, discuss it in the following chapter when I frame an important contrast between pro-gun and pro-control advocates.

MAKES DUBIOUS INFERENCES; FAILS TO ACCEPT
IMPLICATIONS OF HER CLAIMS

Even if the assumptions are plausible, the studies well designed, and the findings potentially revealing, the arguments may range from weak to useless if an author makes dubious inferences from her findings. There are many ways inferences can go wrong. The experimenter may misinterpret the data, or make dubious generalizations from correctly interpreted data. An authority must not only have the ability to identify implications of her assumptions, inferences, and findings, she must be willing to accept them and to adjust her claims accordingly.

With these criteria in hand, we can now use them as indirect ways of determining whether a purported authority is a genuine authority. They will also help us evaluate purported authorities' proffered arguments.

EVALUATING COMPETING EMPIRICAL CLAIMS

Before examining specific claims, let me first address and then set aside a preliminary issue raised at the outset of this chapter: How authoritative are the central players in this debate? By my lights, all key players meet the minimum requirements of expertise. Most work within disciplines that are demonstrably relevant to this debate, namely, criminology, medicine, and public health. All appear to have the requisite degrees and professional standing. The only person whose expertise might not be immediately apparent is John Lott, Jr. The relevance of his discipline to this debate requires explanation. Economists discuss the production, consumption, and transfer of wealth. What does this have to do with guns? The superficial answer is "nothing." What makes economics relevant is that many current economists ply their trade by examining individuals' preferences and the ways in which their preferences influence their behavior. Given that this is relevant to the gun control debate, then we should give economists the benefit of the doubt and acknowledge that Lott has expertise arguably relevant to this issue. None of the main players in this debate is an obvious fraud, even if, as we shall see, some authorities and some authoritative claims are more reliable than others.

Using the previously detailed methods for assessing expertise and the claims of purported experts, I evaluate pro-gun and pro-control empirical arguments, with a special focus on the core pillars of each. Since the NRC Committee's conclusions are largely agnostic, I do not discuss their views separately. Rather, I inject their claims throughout the chapter when they are relevant to my evaluation.

Pro-Gun Arguments

How might we evaluate the pro-gun arguments? For the most part, you will not have to rely upon my bare assessment: I explain my rationale so that you can evaluate my judgments for yourself. I begin by focusing on Kleck's work, especially his claims about the enormous numbers of. I then discuss Lott's claims about the benefits of allowing and encouraging people to carry firearms.

DEFENSIVE GUN USES

As you may recall, based on positive responses from 222 people of the nearly 5,000 people they surveyed, Kleck and Gertz infer that there are 2.5 defensive gun uses per year. This absolute number includes reports of DGUs (a) by everyone in a household (b) during the past five years, and (c) it reflects the researchers' decision to oversample in areas of high gun ownership. Once the researchers adjust for these qualifying factors, they found 56 people who reported that they had used a gun defensively against a potential criminal during the previous year.

There are at least three methodological objections to their survey. None are sufficiently telling to destroy their conclusion; all give us reason for skepticism. Some of these objections have been raised in the literature; others, as far as I can tell, have not.

One, Kleck and Gertz found that slightly more than 1% of the nearly 5,000 people they interviewed claimed to have personally used a gun defensively against a potential criminal in the past year (Kleck, G. and Gertz, M. 1995: table 2 on page 184). They generalized this finding to the entire population. Their inference is based on an affirmative answer by slightly more than one person out of every one hundred people they interviewed. Any inference based on reports of such rare events is dubious. It is easy to see the problem when we think about tests for medically rare conditions. As Hemenway explains:

> With a huge number of actual negatives, virtually any screen will pick up a sizable absolute number of false positives. With few actual positives, it is impossible for a screen to pick up many false

negatives. It follows that, for events with low incidence, random misclassification will result in the estimated incidence being far greater than the true incidence. (Hemenway, D. 1997a: 7)

What this means is that for every chance that Kleck and Gertz might find a false negative report (someone who falsely denies using a gun defensively) there are 99 chances that they could have a false positive (someone who falsely claims to have used a gun defensively) (Hemenway, D. 1997b: 7). To see the difficulty from a different perspective, Kleck and Gertz must explain why more than 96% of people who used a gun defensively mistakenly or falsely denied that use to the NCVS, while pro-control advocates need explain only why less than 1 percent of Kleck-Gertz interviewees mistakenly or falsely reported a DGU. The latter task appears to be easy, while Kleck and Gertz must explain a *massive* mis- or underreporting in the extensive, well-established, and well-regarded NCVS.

The NCVS survey makes it easy enough for interviewees to report DGUs without interviewers encouraging them to concoct, exaggerate, or misremember events (Cook, P. J. 2013: 43). In contrast, the Kleck-Gertz survey arguably encourages subjects to report a DGU by (a) initially announcing the survey's purpose and then (b) asking them directly if they—or someone in their house—used a gun defensively. It encourages what researchers call "personal presentation bias," the desire to make oneself look good (Hemenway, D. 1997a: 8).

The following analogy illustrates the problem: suppose someone wanted to conduct a survey on teenage male sexual behavior. She might use either of two approaches. Using the first, she tells the male teen subjects that she wants to determine how sexually active male teenagers are. She then asks each teenage male if he has had intercourse. A not insignificant number of teenage males would feel uncomfortable admitting to her that they were virgins. On the other approach, the researcher would ask the teenagers open-ended questions about their interpersonal relations. This would permit them to discuss their sexual activity without necessarily encouraging or expecting them to do so. They are not put in a position where they must expressly acknowledge their virginity. To me it seems as if the latter approach is more likely to elicit honest responses.

Second and reinforcing the first, Kleck and Gertz claim that in 86% of the cases the person who answered the phone is the individual in the household who had used a gun defensively. You would have thought that the number would be no more than 50%—especially since children—who are not surveyed—would sometimes answer the phone. Why would the person who had used a gun defensively be *that* much more likely to answer the phone? I see no good explanation. What seems more probable is that if someone were to exaggerate her DGU usage, it would be the person answering the phone; she might be inclined to paint herself as the "hero" of some DGU story. Such a person may not necessarily be consciously lying. He might, for instance, remember a time when he thought he heard someone outside and went for his gun. He then fills out the story—perhaps even to himself—with "what I would have done" under the circumstances.

Three, Kleck and Gertz claim their survey was anonymous and interviewees were told that in advance (Kleck, G. and Gertz, M. 1995: 160). Yet by the time of this survey, if a researcher knew someone's phone number, she could determine the name of the person who lives at that number, and those answering the survey would know that. Setting that problem aside, these researchers said whenever someone reported a DGU, then a supervisor called back to verify her answers. However, to call someone back and be confident that the person verifying the report is the one who made the initial report, then those conducting the survey had to know the identity of the person making the initial report; those reporting a DGU had to know that interviewers knew their identity. This undermines the claim that the survey was anonymous. Yet they claimed their survey was superior to the NCVS since theirs was presumably anonymous.

I suspect these problems—or ones akin to them—explain why few gun researchers accept Kleck's findings that there are 2.5 million DGUs a year. Researchers recently surveyed the first author of every peer-reviewed article on gun control published in the previous five years. Hence, the recipients would be reasonably thought to be experts. Only 8% of those who responded believe there were even 1 million defensive gun uses a year (Hemenway, D. and Nolan, E. P. 2017: survey 18). These results are not skewed because physicians and public health professionals were oversampled. The same percentage of criminologists who filled out the survey (sixteen of seventeen) was equally skeptical (this particular tabulation was not reported in the published study; it was provided courtesy of the author). That show that fewer than 10% of criminologists surveyed think that there are even one million DGUs. That is significant since Kleck had claimed that there were 2.5 million DGUs. The remaining objections to the first pillar of the pro-gun advocates arise from the criteria for assessing putative authorities discussed at the beginning of this chapter.

Lack of Professional Humility

One of the requisite intellectual and moral virtues of a good authority is that she recognizes her own fallibility and exhibits the requisite professional humility. On this measure, Gary Kleck fares badly. I find this regrettable since he has relevant observations to add to this debate. However, as I noted in the last chapter, Kleck does not spend much time rationally challenging pro-control arguments; mainly he blasts or derides gun control advocates. For instance, he states that physicians and public health professionals are rank amateurs employing primitive analytical tools. He also contends that many of them are patently dishonest. He thinks that only a few academics are "genuine experts." The class of experts seems to coincide with those who agree with him.

I find his characterization of other academics not just unbecoming but untenable. As someone who is not a member of any of these disciplines, I am uncomfortable dismissing the works of all members of entrenched academic disciplines, certainly not without convincing evidence of their lack of expertise.

Most of us, and I would have thought this included Kleck, would be loath to think that physicians and medical researchers are scientific amateurs using primitive analytic tools or that they are fundamentally dishonest. Perhaps we put undue faith in physicians and public health workers when we undergo surgery or take medications they prescribe. Still, it seems implausible to think that they are amateurs.

Perhaps though, Kleck thinks that they are amateurs only when studying gun control. However, I cannot imagine a faintly plausible reason for thinking medical researchers can do complex studies to determine the causes of cancer or cures for meningitis or Ebola, yet are completely buffaloed when it comes to designing, running, or interpreting studies on the benefits and dangers of the private ownership of guns. Were their understanding of statistics as outmoded as Kleck claims, why should we embrace their statistical analyses of the safety and efficacy of Epanova (a new drug) or of the latest procedures for an aortic valve replacement?

Nor can I imagine why anyone would think that they are systematically dishonest about gun control studies but scrupulously honest about other matters medical. This is an untenable and dangerous assumption, especially since those he demonizes are in the majority. If these advocates' views were as flawed as he avers, then it should be easy to demonstrate that; therefore, there is no need to demonize them. Finally, although I understand that we should not be reflexively swayed by the majority opinion—whether the topic is moral, philosophical, or scientific—as someone who has often been a minority, in those case, I thought the onus was on me to show that the majority view was mistaken. Merely asserting that they are ignorant, amateurs, or dishonest would have not been respectable, respectful, or productive.

In contrast, I find the gun control advocates are *generally* more academically humble, more likely to acknowledge weaknesses in, and questions about their own claims, and less likely to just dismiss their opponents. That is not to say that there are no pro-control advocates who dismiss pro-gun advocates out of hand. Although a small number will make such a confession in private conversation; they do not publicly *treat* Kleck, Lott, and their ilk as academic pariahs. Since I consider scientific humility a virtue of a purported expert, I am more inclined to believe their findings. If nothing else, someone less prone to categorically dismiss others is less likely to be seriously inconsistent.

My misgivings about Kleck, stemming from his lack of professional humility are amplified once we notice that he is more inclined to be inconsistent and less inclined to see, understand, and accept the implications of his views. Taken together, these factors make me more wary of his claims, even when I am insufficiently knowledgeable to evaluate them directly.

Consistency

Consistency is an important intellectual virtue. Kleck is inconsistent far more often than any genuine authority should be. Throughout his most recent book (2006/1997), but especially in the early chapters, he derides what he dubs "speculation"; elsewhere he calls it "idle speculation." He proclaims, "an ounce of evidence is worth a ton of speculation." This claim is plausible, however, only under a particular rendering of "evidence" and "speculation." If by "evidence" he means "relevant and convincing evidence" and by "speculation" he means "baseless flights of imagination," then his claim is true, albeit trivially so. However, if by "evidence" he means what we ordinarily mean: information that is proffered as evidence, and by "speculation" he means roughly what I meant by "armchair reasoning"—information not expressly dependent on empirical study—then the claim is false. Evidence *is* evidence as framed by armchair reasoning.

Kleck is inconsistent since he lambasts others for using armchair arguments that he uses at every turn. There is nothing wrong with his using armchair reasoning. As I noted, it is necessary for the sound conduct of science. Moreover, on several occasions, he poses plausible armchair objections to others' studies, premises, or inferences. When he does, he is behaving professionally. What *is* objectionable is when others object to his survey's design, or asks whether his assumptions are tenable or his inferences plausible, he is offended and dismisses *their* questions as "idle speculation." Of course if their particular armchair criticisms are faulty, then he is right to object. However, he would be right to object only if they use *flawed* armchair reasoning, not if they use armchair reasoning per se.

Kleck also frequently accuses pro-control advocates of selectively reporting data, of reporting only data that supports their preconceived notions. I would be surprised were that not sometimes true. This is something virtually all of us do, even when we are trying to be honest and fair. Unfortunately he is unwilling to acknowledge that he does the same thing even in cases where his doing so is egregious. For instance, after arguing that international comparisons are illicit, he immediately proceeds to compare gun homicide rates between the United States and Canada. However, if international comparisons are illicit, then they are illicit. What makes the comparison even more inappropriate is that he cherry-picks dates congenial to his views. He begins by noting, "The average 1983-86 homicide rate was 2.6 in Canada and 7.59 in the United States, yielding a ratio of 2.92 . . . . after Canada implemented more stringent gun controls, its homicide rate advantage over the United States actually decreased" (1997/2006: 360). I did not check his figures; I take him at this word. However, I did check the most recent figures from 2009, when the Canadian homicide rate was 1.7—a 40% decline from the figure he used. During the same period, the US homicide rate had also declined, but by less than 30%. The so-called advantage of which he boasted had vanished.

To make matters worse, he glides over the obvious fact that Canada's homicide rate is less than a third that of the Unites States. That is a huge difference. I am not sure why he thinks this example demonstrates the benefits of the US approach to gun ownership and gun control. I wonder what he would count as evidence against the value of the private ownership of guns.

I want to mention another tension in his view, even if it is not an outright inconsistency. In several places Kleck emphatically states that criminals who carry guns show a greater intent to harm their victims (1997/2006: 217, 229) He contends that anyone who denies this claim is ignoring common sense. "The ordinary commonsensical interpretation of human behavior is that most of what people do they intend to do, and that most of the effects directly produced by their actions, they intended to produce" (1997/2006: 230).

At the same time, Kleck maintains that criminals who carry guns are *less* likely to harm their victims (1997/2006: 218). Although these claims are not outright contradictory, neither are they comfortable bedfellows. If gun-toting criminals are more intent on harming their victims, then given what he dubs the commonsense notion of "intent," we would expect that armed criminals would more likely harm their victims. It seems we must either reject the commonsense notion of "intent" or reject his claim that gun-toting criminals are more intent on harming their victims. To make matters worse for this argument, if criminals armed with firearms are less likely to harm victims, then on the face of it, this appears to be a benefit of having armed criminals. Of course it would be better were there no criminals are all. However, if he is correct, it is arguably safer for criminals to carry firearms rather than knives or baseball bats since, when they do, they are less likely to harm their victims.

I say these claims are in tension rather than contradictory since, with verbal gymnastics and conceptual gerrymandering, we might make them compatible. However, barring such gerrymandering, the combined claims do not fit. However, I wanted to mention it here, not just because it is another instance of his inconsistency, but because this point undergirds an argument I offer in the last chapter.

Failure to Trace, Appreciate, and Accept Implications of His claims

The remaining problems arise from Kleck's failure to trace, appreciate, and then accept plausible implications of his views. Three are not very serious problems but do merit mention. The last two are quite serious, sufficient, I think, to throw considerable doubt on his DGU claims.

One, in several places, Kleck and Lott claim that most victims of gunshot wounds are themselves criminals, usually drug dealers (1997/2006: 236). However, were that true, then it would follow that law-abiding citizens are less likely to need firearms for self-defense against a criminal. If so, then why do these pro-gun advocates put so much emphasis on putting guns into law-abiding citizens' hands?

Two, Kleck acknowledges that a significant number of criminals get their guns by stealing them from law-abiding citizens (1997/ 2006: 90-93), yet he seems to forget this fact when evaluating gun control proposals. Instead, he continually claims that measures denying criminals the ability to own guns have the untoward effect of denying law-abiding citizens the ability to obtain guns for self-defense. Of course if a number of criminals get their guns from law-abiding citizens—as he acknowledges—then gun control measures will indirectly limit some criminals' access to guns. This should be counted as a benefit of gun control.

Three, in several places, Kleck claims if murderers and robbers do not have access to handguns, then many will use more lethal weapons. If we ban handguns, they will resort to long guns (1997/ 2006: 366). He also claims criminals are deterred from attacking someone they think might be armed. I would be surprised were both claims not occasionally true. However, were both *generally* true, then having more armed citizens would lead criminals to resort to more lethal weapons. Barring that, they may preemptively shoot the victim before the victim can defend herself, or they will "hunt" with armed accomplices. Were either of these true, then that appears to undermine the supposed unqualified value of having a large number of armed private citizens.

Four, some gun control advocates claim that criminals not infrequently take guns from people who try to use them defensively and then use those guns against them. Kleck claims this happens rarely—in roughly 1% of the cases (Kleck, G. 1997/2006: 169). He offers this figure to reassure gun owners. However, it should not reassure them if his claims about DGUs are accurate. If there are 2.5 million DGUs annually and in 1% of these cases, the criminal takes the owner's gun and uses it again him, then we can infer from his findings that 25,000 defenders will have their guns used against them each year. Either he should revisit his DGU estimates or else acknowledge that the prospects of having one's gun used against oneself is substantial.

Five, the same survey that shows that there are 2.5 million DGUs annually finds that those who use guns defensively claim they "certainly or almost certainly saved" 400,000 lives (Kleck, G. 1997/ 2006: 174). This looks like an attractive pro-gun inference. It is not. Here's why. We have two options. Either Kleck's DGU estimates are *wildly* off or our country's murder rate, which is already magnitudes higher than that of all other developed countries, would have been nearly thirty times higher! Since no country in the world has a murder rate that high, we have good reason to doubt Kleck's DGU estimates. Or, if his estimates and the interviewee's predictions are even remotely accurate, then we have ironclad evidence that the United States has the world's most violent citizens.

Together these features make me leery of accepting many of Kleck's claims. Moreover, the last two points give us independent reasons for rejecting his claims about DGUs. Since this is a core pillar of the pro-gun empirical argument and a component of arguments for an instrumental right to bear arms, then these findings further tip the scales in favor of heightened gun control.

THE BENEFITS OF SHALL-ISSUE CARRY LAWS

John Lott claims that if states must issue carry permits to all citizens except former felons and certifiably mentally ill people, then there will be dramatic declines in homicides and other violent crimes. His studies find that "for every 1,000 additional people with permits, there are 0.3 fewer murders, 2.4 fewer rapes, 21 fewer robberies, and 14.1 fewer aggravated assaults" (2010/2000/1997: 3013).

I later canvas specific methodological objections to Lott's views. I delay raising them until I first address general worries about research like Lott's that relies so heavily on complex statistical manipulation. As you may recall, I explained in the previous chapter that the NAS report claimed that we need considerable study before we can make reliable claims about DGUs, carry laws, and the effectiveness of various gun control measures. What is intriguing is that in an appendix to that report, one of the authors mounts a powerful critique of the Committee's finding. Horowitz does not deny that we need more study of gun ownership and control. What he doubts is whether these studies' successes will depend on their authors' using more complex and sophisticated statistics (2004).

In raising this objection, Horowitz reflects a significant trend in the field. An increasing number of statisticians have become wary of the common use of statistics to undergird empirical solutions to complex policy issues like gun control. This point cuts against many studies, both pro-control and pro-gun. Noted statistician David Freedman explains the difficulty. Researchers begin by embracing the common belief that any adequate statistical model must control for relevant variables. Unfortunately, researchers often do not know which factors are relevant. Even when they do know, trying to adequately control for potentially confounding factors requires making two dubious assumptions: (a) the variables play the same role in all circumstances, and (b) each factor is related linearly (so, e.g., as the number of households with guns increases by x%, then the number homicides increases by x%). Unfortunately, without deep reservoirs of knowledge—which, if we had, might well make the research superfluous—we never know in advance that either, let alone both, assumption(s) is (are) true. How could we? This is precisely the information we are trying to ascertain with the experiments. Freedman claims that the common statistical solution to this well-known problem is circular. Once "breakdowns in assumptions are detected, [then] ... the model is redefined to accommodate. In short, hiding the problems can become a major goal of model building" (Freedman 2010: 12). The result is that the models claiming to prove a significant causal claim "generally turn out to depend on a series of untested, even unarticulated, technical assumptions" that have been jerry-rigged so that the study yields the result that the experimenter wanted when she began the study (2010: 12).

This leads to a further and more serious, difficulty noted by both Freedman and Horowitz: the way the model is constructed and the "data are selected introduces uncertainty" (Freedman, D. A. 2010: 21). The standard statistical procedures are effective if we can assume adequate numbers of subjects and a genuinely random sample. The problem is that "the data in hand are simply [those] . . . most readily available" (2010: 22). Likely more worrisome, researchers assume that each controlled variable is wholly independent of all others: changes in one variable will not cause (or be caused by) changes in another variable (or pairs of variables). However, "dependence [between variables] is the rule rather than the exception . . . even fairly modest amounts of dependence can create substantial bias in estimated standard errors" (2010: 26). This is a general problem of all studies of crime, not just the issue of gun control. "The independence assumption is fragile. It is fragile as an empirical matter because real world criminal justice processes are unlikely to produce data for which independence can be reasonably assumed. (Indeed, if independence were the rule, criminal justice researchers would have little to study)" (2010: 28).

Together these factors explain the problem of putting so much weight on using bare statistics to resolve these problems, even when using sophisticated "regression analyses":

> I do not think that regression can carry much of the burden in a causal argument. Nor do regression equations, by themselves, give much help in controlling for confounding variables. Arguments based on statistical significance of coefficients seem generally suspect; so do causal interpretations of coefficients. . . . [T]echnical fixes do not solve the problems, which are at a deeper level. (Freedman 2010: 44)

In sum, the kinds of statistics used by both Kleck and Lott— and especially Lott—make a big to do about employing regression analyses. Doing so does not assuage Freedman's concerns. They "are not a particularly good way of doing empirical work in the social sciences today, because the technique depends on knowledge that we do not have" (the factors mentioned above) (2010: 54). They are "seldom if ever reliable for causal inference" (2010: 58). Statistics are simply no substitute for effort and "shoe leather." One has to look for evidence and then test hypotheses in the real world—a suggestion that undergirds some of my policy proposals in the final chapter.

It is not merely that reliance on these statistics is itself dubious, their use—especially by Lott—is at odds with one of the key dispositions we expect in experts. Genuine experts should be able to explain their methodology, their findings, and their inferences clearly. None of the authors is demonstrably unclear in the sense that their prose is murky. However, especially in light of the previous critiques, I have considerable question about the clarity of Lott's methodology. His studies are difficult to assess since they depend on high-level statistical methods and complex rationales for his guiding methodological assumptions. When others question his assumptions and methodologies, he responds by tinkering with those assumptions and trotting out even more complex statistical jargon. This is not scientifically becoming.

Horowitz helps explain my concern. Someone like Lott will have difficulty properly specifying his models; this shows "there is little likelihood that persuasive conclusions about the effects of right-to-carry laws can be drawn from analyses of observational (nonexperimental) data" (Horowitz, J. L. 2004: 299). The explanation of this claim is complicated; it unfolds in two stages. The first springs from the framework within which causal explanations must be made:

The fundamental problem in measuring the effect of a right-to-carry law . . . is that at any given time and place, a right-to-carry law is either in effect or not in effect. Therefore, one can measure the crime rate with the law in effect or without it, depending on the state of affairs at the time and place of interest, but not both with and without the law [at the same time]. Consequently, one of the two measurements needed to implement the definition of the law's effect is always missing. (Horowitz, J. L. 2004: 299–300)

There are two principal obstacles to identifying the relevant causes and effects. One, "factors that affect crime other than adoption of a right-to-carry law may change between" those years. Among other things, crime tends to move in relatively inexplicable waves. Moreover, "states that have right-to-carry laws in effect in a given year may be systematically different from the states that do not have these laws" (Horowitz, J. L. 2004: 300). Second, although we may know what some variables affecting crime rates are, we cannot assume—as Freedman noted—that these variables play the same roles, to the same degree, in different cities, counties, states, regions, or countries (Horowitz, J. L. 2004: 305). For example, poverty may play a significant explanatory role in states with low and porous safety nets; it may not play much of a role in states with robust safety nets.

We also find a number of more specific methodological objections to Lott in the pro-control literature. Although more specific, they are in the same vein as the objections raised by Freedman and Horowitz. The most common critique is that the statistical models on which Lott's surveys are built are deeply flawed. His conclusions depend entirely on miniscule differences in the model's specifications (what they measure, how they measure it, and what they construe the findings as revealing). Some took Lott's findings and slightly altered the specifications (e.g., which counties are excluded from the analysis); others modified the specifications by limiting the categories of crime (they claim nine categories are too many: the numbers within each group are too small to be statistically significant); still others claimed that he used too many (thirty-six) geographical control variables (age, gender, location, size of town, etc.), especially since (recall Freedman) many of these variables are interdependent. Regardless of which changes the researchers made, all found that under *minimally* different conditions, the reported enormous benefits of shall-issue laws vanished.

Moreover, Lott and Mustard's (1997) initial findings occur primarily because they began studying carry laws during the years in which there was a notable upsurge in violent crime and ended at the point when violent crime was on the wane. Their choice of dates skews the data in their favor (Ayres, I. and Donohue, J. J., III 2003: 1216-1217). Nonetheless, Ayers and Donohue argue, if we use proper model specifications, "shall-issue laws were associated with statistically significant *higher* crime rates in eight of the nine crime categories" (1223; emphasis mine).

Perhaps all Lott's methodological moves are legitimate, although the previous criticisms suggest that they are not. However, independently of his arguments' rational force, one thing is clear. Those who cite him when preaching the gun gospel (Lott 3:16), do not have reason to think his methodology is appropriate and his findings revealing. I know a fair bit about statistics. If I cannot follow some of his intricate explanations, then I am confident that the average NRA member or those who rely on FOX News cannot either. That does not mean that Lott is mistaken. What it does mean is those who cite him approvingly do not have any evidence that what he says is accurate or authoritative. It is simply that he says what they want to hear. The same goes for the avid gun philosophers discussed in chapter 4. They cite his conclusions, but none that I mention explain his methodology or consider critiques of him, not even those offered by the agnostic study conducted by the National Research Council (Hall, T. 2006; Huemer, M. 2003; Hunt, L. H. 2011; Wheeler, S. C., III 1997, 2001; Stell, L. 2001).

Since we have no direct evidence for what he claims, and his exposition is often murky, we must look at elements of his arguments we can follow and then judge his relative expertise by comparing the clarity and persuasiveness of his argument with the clarity of arguments offered by the NRC and by the advocates of serious gun control. I do not think that Lott fares well in such a comparison.

In addition to the above methodological objections, the analysis of expertise earlier in the chapter highlights one other important problem with accepting Lott's findings. He does not seem to see, and therefore, could not possibly accept, one inference from his findings. He claims that "for every 1,000 additional people with permits, there are 0.3 fewer murders, 2.4 fewer rapes, 21 fewer robberies, and 14.1 fewer aggravated assaults" (2010/2000/ 1997: 3013). He also claims that the benefits of shall-issue laws are *cumulative* and *linear*: the more permits we issue immediately or over time, the greater the benefits. If we accept his findings and this explicit assumption, then we can predict that if we issued 1 million permits in each state, then more than two-thirds of all states would not have a single homicide. If we issued 1.2 million permits throughout the combined six northeastern states, then there would not be a single homicide in that area of the country— although that region has nearly 18% of the US population. These claims are implausible.

Pro-Control Arguments

As I mentioned earlier, the central pillar of the pro-control argument is the general association between private gun ownership and various forms of harm (homicides, suicides, accidents, etc.). These correlations are especially striking and troublesome when we look at children and law enforcement officers. In the United States, children "are thirteen times more likely to die from a firearm homicide . . . than children in comparable developed nations" (Miller, M., Azrael, D., and Hemenway, D. 2013: 536). We should protect our children, not put them in harm's way. We should likewise be concerned that law enforcement "officers in the high-gun states had 3 times the likelihood of being killed compared with low-gun states" (Swedler, D. I. et al. 2015: 2047). Being a law enforcement officer is dangerous in all circumstances. We should not make it worse. Perhaps neither fact is best explained by the higher prevalence of guns. However, these are findings that should be explained, and the increased presence of guns is a plausible candidate.

Especially since, as you may recall, the National Research Council's Committee found that the association between gun prevalence and violence is well-established (Wellford, C. F., Pepper, J. V., and Petrie, C. V. 2004: 6). So barring overpowering evidence to the contrary, this is a claim that ordinary people can reasonably embrace. That correlation is visible when we compare states, countries, and regions within the United States. The homicide rate in the South—which has the highest gun prevalence—is 45.9 per 100,000, while the more densely populated Northeast (with low gun prevalence) has a homicide rate of 12.4 (Federal Bureau of Investigation 2017: table 3). We should not ignore the statistical problems mentioned earlier: there may be other factors at play (for instance, relative poverty is higher and the social safety net is more porous in the South). However, it is difficult to believe that the higher number of households with guns and the *much weaker* gun control laws are not part of any viable explanation of these findings.

Pro-gun advocates think that pro-control advocates make too much of this association, especially when control advocates base their claims—as they do in part—on international comparisons. Gun advocates usually acknowledge that the United States has a much higher private gun ownership rate and a much higher homicide rate than similarly developed countries. What they dispute is these two factors are causally connected. They offer various armchair arguments to explain why the correlation does not show causation. This is a wholly legitimate use of armchair arguments. The question is whether their explanations are more plausible than those offered by pro-control advocates.

The most common alternative explanation is that economically similar European countries are more homogeneous than the United States. The idea is this: since their citizens are more alike, then there is less violence in general and homicide in specific. This is a sensible supposition. Nonetheless, we have reason to doubt whether this could explain the enormous disparity in homicide rates between the United States, Europe, Australia, and Canada. Many of these societies, and especially Canada, are culturally diverse. Canada has not only large Asian and Middle Eastern populations, but it also has a significant division between the English-speaking majority and the French-speaking minority. Despite its vast cultural diversity, the homicide rate there is one-third that of the United States. Canada has much stricter gun laws and, consequently, far fewer privately owned guns. Pro-gun advocates' armchair suggestion, although initially plausible, appears to clash with the evidence, at least that from Canada.

Others gun advocates, like Lott, raise more methodological objections to international comparisons: since there is no single international body studying private gun ownership across countries, then there is no way to determine relative gun prevalence (2010/ 2000/1997: 1913). Others, like Kleck, just note there has always been large disparities in both private gun ownership and homicide rates, and therefore, for no specifically proffered reason, we cannot fruitfully compare other countries with the United States (1997/ 2006: 253). I find both explanations odd. First, although there are problems with international comparisons of private gun ownership, I see no reason to think these are significant enough to explain the enormous disparity in homicide rates in the United States relative to other developed countries. Two, if international comparisons are illicit, then any findings in the United States would not be applicable to other developed countries. Three, I do not understand the relevance of Kleck's observation.

Kopel offers a different explanation, the details of which vary depending on the country in question. For instance, he claims that Japan's homicide rates is lower because it has large numbers of police who are highly respected, even idolized, by the country's civilians (1992: 150-468). In Great Britain, the explanation is political. While British gun enthusiasts were open to discussing various forms of gun control, "Gun advocates in the U.S. were more aggressive and less interested in compromise" (1992: 1122). What is common to all these cases is Kopel's claim that gun control advocates ignore the ways that "gun controls fit into the rest of the society's culture" (1992: 63). In particular, "Americans do not trust authority as much as most citizens of the British Commonwealth and Japan do." I think he is right that Americans do fear government more than do citizens of most other developed countries. What is debatable is whether this fear is well-founded. Moreover, even if it is, it is not obvious why that is a reason for rejecting moderate or even serious gun control.

That, though, leads to a secondary line of argumentation by pro-gun advocates: even if control is abstractly justified, none of the specific proposals will save that many lives. That is why Kleck spends considerable energy attacking specific proposals. He claims, for example, that *relatively* few people are killed by any particular type of weapon, for example, Saturday night specials or assault weapons. Consequently, banning any one of these particular weapons is unlikely to save large numbers of people. Moreover, requiring guns to be registered might keep firearms out of the hands of some criminals, but certainly not all, particularly not those who are determined to obtain firearms. In a society like ours, there are too many alternative sources. Criminals can steal them, obtain them from a family member or friend, or purchase them on the black market. Does this provide a compelling reason for doubting the efficacy of gun control?

It might. But probably not. The results of each measure in isolation may well be small. However, if we implemented them not one-by-one but as a coordinated phalanx of gun policies, the results might well be significant. The problem is that although this seems like a promising armchair solution, we do not have, and are unlikely to have, strong empirical evidence that this strategy would be efficacious. Why? We are unlikely to implement these coordinated measures in tandem in any single US jurisdiction, let alone in enough jurisdictions to have the robust number of subjects we need to justify strong conclusions. The chance of finding *definitive* empirical evidence that a coordinated array of gun control policies will work in the United States is slim to none. However, this sets the bar too high. The political difficulty of implementing regulations should not undermine efforts that might indirectly reveal the benefits of gun control. Why can we not implement some policies in some districts and others in different districts, and, in each, see if the homicide rate declines. If it does, we cannot confidently say that the decline would have been greater were all policies implemented in the same place at the same time. Nonetheless, the evidence could suggest that might well be true.

Moreover, we have indirect evidence supporting this supposition. Since we have a highly plausible link between gun prevalence and homicide rates, then we have reason to think that gun control measures that keep some guns out of some people's hands will likely lower homicide rates. It will not eliminate homicide. No one has ever said or thought *that*. In the same way, no one ever claimed or thought that lowering speed limits, requiring new cars to have air bags, and requiring drivers to wear seat belts would each, on its own, eliminate all—or even substantial numbers of—automobile deaths. However, advocates did think that these measures *in concert* would lessen the number of automobile deaths and serious injuries. They were right (Insurance Institute for Highway Safety 2015).

Admittedly, this evidence is not unassailable. It might be that there are other features of a society that explain both gun prevalence and homicide rates. However, sans alternative explanations more compelling than those previously offered, the core pillar of pro-control advocates stands firm. There are reasons to think control cannot only decrease homicides and suicides, it can also diminish the general social dis-ease created by the fear of gun violence (Cook, P. J. and Ludwig, J. 2002: 541).

Despite the highly suggestive empirical evidence, the NRC is right: beyond the core fact of the broad correlation between gun prevalence and gun violence, many specific empirical claims of pro-control advocates are not definitive. We *do* need more, and more serious, empirical work.

What should we do in the meantime?

Chapter 8

Why We Need Gun Control

We began this inquiry seeking clear, definitive answers to three distinct but related questions:

- *Whom* should we permit to own guns?
- *Which* firearms should we allow them to own?
- *How* should we restrict (a) the times and ways people can purchase and sell them, (b) the times (if any) when (some) owners can carry them, and (c) the ways owners must store them?

If our aspiration was to find incontrovertible answers to these questions, our hope has been dashed. The armchair arguments tend to support at least moderate gun control; however, these arguments were insufficient to settle the issue. Arguments for an instrumental right to arms have some argumentative purchase but are far short of what advocates aver or want. Finally, the empirical evidence, although suggestive, is far from unassailable. It does reveal a connection between homicides and gun ownership; it also undermines the strongest claims made on behalf of owning—and especially carrying—guns. We must decide how to proceed on less than unassailable evidence.

Before beginning to mount a more sustained argument for serious gun control, I must carefully consider an argument I first raised in chapter 2: the social costs of enforcing any significant constraints on private ownership of guns would be intolerable. The nature of this argument is not that these costs would be too high inasmuch as they deprive people of a source of enjoyment or an effective right to self-defense—although pro-gun advocates also believe that. This argument purportedly shows that serious control is wrong even if the standardly identified costs of owning guns (homicides, suicides, etc.) exceed its putative benefits (e.g., enhanced self-defense).

THE COSTS OF CRIMINALIZATION AND ENFORCEMENT

The issue is both general and specific: it is general inasmuch as it identifies reasons against making any activity illegal. It is specific inasmuch as there are particular reasons for worrying about making the private ownership of guns mostly or entirely illegal. The general argument has two prongs. One, instances of virtually every human action can, and likely do, occasionally cause harm. If the mere possibility of harm were grounds for criminalizing an action, then we would criminalize every action. That is a nonstarter. An action should have more than a faint possibility of causing harm to justify criminalizing it. Two, there are costs of making any action illegal, including acts we all agree ought to be illegal (e.g., homicide). I discussed many of these in chapter 2. We should not ignore these costs. They are sufficiently potent that we need good reason to make any action illegal. The burden is always on the state that wants to make an action illegal. The burden can be met. In this case, we need reason to make the purchase, sales, and private ownership of guns largely or entirely illegal.

I earlier suggested that this debate appears to resemble one about Prohibition nearly a century ago. In 1920, the United States prohibited "the manufacture, sale, or transportation of intoxicating liquors within, the importation . . . into, or the exportation . . . from" the United States. This constitutional provision stayed in effect for thirteen years until it was repealed. Why was it passed? I suspect there were two reasons, one plausible and the other not so much. The plausible one was that even though many people like to consume alcohol, a sufficiently large minority of these people do not drink responsibly; the human, medical, and financial costs of alcoholism are enormous. If we can prevent these costs, then surely we should. Prohibition appeared to be a sensible way of achieving these noble ends. The not-so-good—and likely the real—reason for its passage was religious and not secular. Many religious citizens thought consuming alcohol was a sin.

Regardless of the real or possible reasons for its passage, the cost of the law was high. Many people liked to consume alcohol. When it became illegal, criminals stepped in to satisfy that demand. This led to a significant crime wave and frequent gangland violence over control of the illegal distribution of liquor. Finally, citizens had had enough. They repealed the amendment. Pro-gun advocates might claim that any attempt to ban guns would fail for the same reasons that Prohibition failed. At first glance, this seems like a plausible suggestion.

First glances can be deceiving. There *are* lessons we can and should learn from this comparison. This historical example does show why we should not make a highly popular activity illegal willy-nilly. However, Prohibition was not "alcohol control." It *banned* its sale and transportation. It made it impossible for anyone to legally have or consume alcohol unless she made it herself on her own property.

When Americans repealed Prohibition, they did not thereby eliminate state control on the purchase, consumption, and transportation of alcohol. I would be shocked if there were any jurisdictions where people can, even now, legally purchase alcohol 24 hours a day, seven days a week. In most jurisdictions, it cannot be purchased until later in the day on Sunday nor can it be sold (without a waiver) within a specified distance (often 100 feet) of an elementary school or a church. Minors cannot purchase alcohol—although what counts as a minor may vary from jurisdiction to jurisdiction. Drivers cannot consume more than a couple of drinks before driving. Do these myriad mini-bans and regulations make alcohol illegal? No, inasmuch as adults can still purchase and consume alcohol, the current regime is not an alcohol ban. However, inasmuch as one cannot purchase booze at 6 am on a Sunday of if she is twelve-years-old, and she cannot have four drinks in the two hours before driving, then we still ban some people from having alcohol and we control its sale, purchase, and use for all people. Among other things, we tax it at a higher rate than we do almost all consumer goods. The income from these taxes helps defray some social costs of alcoholism.

Although these myriad laws are not generally described as "alcohol bans," someone might get sufficiently worked up so that she construes these measures as bans. I think many of these controls are entirely reasonable (making drunk driving illegal); some I don't think are especially reasonable (I cannot buy beer early Sunday morning). However, why get irate about this minor legal restriction since, with minimal planning, I do not need to purchase beer during those hours? In my view, these latter rules are vestiges of an older age, and, even if unreasonable, they are merely annoyances, not grist for a revolutionary mill.

None of the widely discussed and viable gun control measures is analogous to Prohibition. They are not gun bans. They are bans *for certain people* (children and former violent felons), bans *on certain weapons* (bazookas and mortars), and controls on firearms that people may legitimately own. Hence, arguments against Prohibition are not arguments against these familiar forms of gun control.

Although the impetus for this argument hits at something important, we should be careful lest this line of reasoning inappropriately sways us. The fact that people dislike a law may make the costs of enforcing the law high, sometimes formidably high. We should consider that when judging its relative costs and benefits. However, there are two problems with letting this consideration always carry the argumentative day.

First, sometimes we should do what is right, no matter how much people are offended by it. I can think of three cases where even though a judicial decision or statutory law offended a sizeable portion of the population, the government acted rightly in passing and enforcing that law. One, a majority of white Southerners objected to laws and court decisions banning segregation and requiring that minorities have equal voting rights. However, that gave us no reason to let segregation stand or to deny African Americans the right to vote. Two, the government rightly banned leaded gasoline to protect public health, even though that increased the cost of gasoline and thereby angered or inconvenienced many citizens. The ban required oil companies to spend more money further refining oil rather than simply adding lead—a cheap method of raising gasoline's octane (crucial for the smooth functioning of an internal combustion engine). However, adding lead to gasoline meant that these engines belched huge quantities of this dangerous metal into the atmosphere. Three, many people initially complained when the government required new autos to have seats belts, and later when it required drivers and passengers to wear them. Many people thought wearing seat belts was uncomfortable and inconvenient, a violation of their right to choose. The state saved many lives by enforcing both these laws, people's objections notwithstanding. In all three cases, although there were initially significant objections to government action, most people eventually accepted the new practices; now virtually everyone takes them for granted. Most people understand that implementing them was wise.

We have a second reason to worry about allowing people's objections to a law to scupper that law. Announcing that we will consider citizens' displeasure when deciding whether to pass (or enforce) a law will motivate some people to manufacture or artificially inflate their discontent. If I think the state might not institute a law if I and others find it very offensive, then I have a reason to be as vociferous as possible in my condemnation of it. However, I should not be able to get my way by making myself the squeakiest wheel.

These considerations explain why the analogy with Prohibition is not telling against most actual gun control proposals. Nonetheless, the analogy may be telling against hypothetical ones. In a county like the United States, where so many private citizens own guns, anything approximating a gun ban would have enormous, and probably insurmountable, enforcement costs. Prohibition created a cycle of crime and violence that almost devoured the country. We should not make this mistake again. Even if *complete* gun control were the most sensible approach abstractly, we have good reason not to ban guns in the United States. The widespread prevalence of gun ownership and many American's desire to own firearms erects powerful obstacles to gun bans that cannot be overcome soon or even in the foreseeable future. We should not even try. We should aim lower.

Of course, most proposals do aim lower. They ban some small subclasses of people from owning guns. They ban ownership of *some* firearms and *some* bullets. They specify that we should have extensive background checks of aspiring gun owners. They want to ban transfers of guns from legitimate to illegitimate owners. None of these common proposals resemble Prohibition. They are more akin to current restrictions on the sale and consumption of alcohol. Some people cannot purchase it at all. Those who can purchase it can do so only from certain stores at certain times. No one can carry open bottles of alcohol in our autos or consume it in many public parks or government buildings ("no booze zones"). Although some people may not like these restrictions, the reaction to them is nothing like people's revulsion to Prohibition. This offers some guidance about the proper ways of thinking about gun control.

In short, although the analogy might be telling against gun bans, since the United States has not and will not seriously consider such bans, the analogy is not instructive. Even if it were, ardent gun control advocates might contend that gun bans were akin to rules requiring people to wear seat belts. People may vociferously complain now, but eventually, they will get over it. I am not convinced. However, since the rules actually advocated are well shy of a ban, we can safely put this argument to rest. We should instead address the genuine questions about gun control and gun ownership that people actually forward. We must reassess these proposals in light of the best arm-chair and empirical arguments. The first step is isolating competing assumptions guiding pro-gun and the pro-control proposals. Once we grasp these differences, we can identify critical problems with policies that encourage extensive private ownership of guns.

IDENTIFYING DIFFERENT GUIDING ASSUMPTIONS

Pro-gun advocates and pro-control advocates standardly embrace different views about the proper role of government, the nature of human motivation, and the common causes of harm. Those who avidly defend a serious right to bear arms are typically skeptical of the intentions and actions of the government (Wheeler, S. C., III 1997, 2001; Kopel, D. B. 1992), while those who defend serious gun control are more inclined to trust government. The former, following President Reagan, often describe government as "the problem"; the latter think government is a viable, and often the only, way to address serious social problems (Amy, D. 2007). For instance, pro-control advocates think we need government to protect citizens from polluted air and water; tainted food; dangerous chemicals in paints, cleansers, cosmetics, and toiletries; badly designed consumer products (baby cribs with wide slats or dangerous toys); dangerous or ineffective medications or health supplements; and unsafe workplaces. They also think governments should play a crucial role in constraining gun violence.

Pro-gun advocates and pro-control advocates also understand human motivation differently and often explain human violence differently. Gun advocates assume most humans, including most criminals, are rational calculators. People chose how to act based largely, if not exclusively, on their assessment of the costs and benefits of available alternatives. Each person identifies what she understands to be her choices, predicts the likely outcome of acting on each, and then chooses the one with the best prudential outcome. Given this motivational assumption, the best way to control violent crime is to create an environment in which more potential criminals judge that the costs of committing violent crimes are too high. Gun advocates contend that arming citizens is the most effective way of doing that. A potential robber will be deterred from entering a house if she thinks the owners are home and armed (Kleck); she will be disinclined to stick-up someone on the street if she thinks the potential victim is packing (Lott). No other strategy is as likely to diminish violent criminal behavior. Gun control measures would have few benefits and significant deleterious consequences. By limiting the criminal's access to handguns, they prompt criminals to resort to more lethal weapons, for instance, long guns (Kleck, G. 1997/2006: 136). By limiting law-abiding citizen's access to firearms, we deny them the means of warding off criminal predators.

That an economist like Lott and a criminologist like Kleck construe humans as rational calculators is understandable. That is a staple of modern economic analyses and much of criminology (Cornish, D. B. and Clarke, R. V. 1987; Hasman, D. 2012).

However, many academics now think that rational choice theory is unable to explain much human behavior (Kahneman, D. 2011).

Humans simply are not the conscious calculators we sometimes think we are. Most people have a flawed sense of who they are, what they want, and why they act as they do (Dunning, D. 2005; Dunning, D., Heath, C., and Suls, J. M. 2005; Ehrlinger, J., Gilovich, T., and Ross, L. 2005; Festinger, L. 1957; Hansford, B. C. and Hattie, J. A. 1982; Kolar, D. W., Funder, D. C., and Colvin, C. R. 1996; Pronin, E. 2009; Pronin, E., Lin, D. Y., and Ross, L. 2002; Tavris, C. and Aronson, E. 2007; Tversky, A. and Kahneman, D. 1973, 1974; Wilson, T. D. 2004). If these thinkers are correct when describing the actions of ordinary people, their claims are even more likely true of common criminals who are, on average, noticeably less intelligent than the average citizen (Ellis, L. and Walsh A. 2003: 344).

Pro-control advocates tend to agree with these thinkers. They believe that a significant portion of human behavior—including much aberrant behavior—is not the result of conscious, rational deliberation; they thereby reject a key guiding assumption of pro-gun supporters. They acknowledge that some violent crime is borne of conscious malice. It is just that they think much of it springs from familiar, but less deliberative, engines of human behavior: anger, drunkenness, lack of care, weak will, the lack of foresight, rotten luck, and accidents. These common causes of behavior explain much harm, especially when people engage in inherently dangerous activities like owning firearms. I think it is folly to deny the powerful role these mundane human frailties play in causing violence (LaFollette, H. 2017). Yet this is precisely what most pro-gun advocates do, if not expressly, at least by their silence.

Pro-control advocates' contend that many gun deaths are more like most drowning deaths and lethal auto accidents. Most automobile deaths and injuries occur because one or both drivers were tired, busy, distracted, inobservant, annoyed, depressed, in a rush, or inebriated. Few people drown because someone tried to drown them intentionally. Most people drown because they were careless, showing off, failed to understand their physical limitations, or misjudged the depth of the water or the speed of the current (Erdman, J. 2015).

Likewise, as I noted earlier, a number of homicides occur because of human error, lack of care, impulsiveness, or because the killer is angry or jealous. Inasmuch as this *is* true, then we have a serious chance of controlling the number of deaths by firearms by deploying a public health approach to gun violence. In contrast, we cannot do much to stop psychopaths or sociopaths except by having a better police force and a more robust mental health system.

Of course, even if we acknowledge the wisdom of the prohealth approach, we must still decide how to best pursue it. As I explained in the previous chapter, there are insurmountable practical obstacles to obtaining empirical evidence that *definitively* establishes that any set of gun control proposals is effective, let alone superior to all others. However, why do we think that is required before we can proceed? We can and should use the tried and true method of "muddling through."

A STRATEGY

Freedman claims that our inability to find definitive evidence does not result from failing to adequately manipulate available data. Using more sophisticated statistical techniques will not resolve this policy debate. He argues that, as with all public policy debates, we must rely on "shoe leather" and "natural experiments." I think Freedman's (and Horowitz's) suggestions parallel advice Charles Lindbloom offered to government administrators half a century ago. "Theorists often ask the administrator to go the long way round to the solution of his problems . . . when the administrator knows that the best available theory will work less well than more modest incremental comparisons" (1959: 87).

Lindbloom's proposal for "muddling through" looks akin to a proposal I made near the end of the previous chapter. We have armchair arguments bolstered by empirical evidence suggesting that gun control can be beneficial. True, the NRC Committee found that evidence for any specific proposal is thin. I explained why that will not—indeed cannot—change. Nonetheless, we can use the evidence we do have to frame a series of "natural experiments." We can implement the most promising policies in different cities, states, and counties, and see what happens. If homicides, suicides, or accidents decline, we cannot straightforwardly infer that the policy caused the improvement; if the rate does not decline, we cannot necessarily infer that the policy failed. Despite these limitations, we take the evidence we obtain and make policy baby steps. We can use this strategy as individuals frequently do. We cannot confidently predict whether to request a raise, what would be the best college major, where to invest our retirement funds, whom to date, and for whom to vote. We make educated but imperfect predictions from available data and act accordingly. Sometimes our actions misfire and we change course. Sometime they appear to work and we continue on the same track. Since the policies we are discussing are not bans but rather forms of control (akin to myriad controls on alcohol), then we need not worry that these experiments will thereby violate some serious right to bear arms. None are bans, and some of these are—or are close policy cousins of—proposals gun advocates themselves make or are committed to making.

More relevant to the current debate, this is what governments normally do when developing and implementing policies. It was the strategy we used to promote automobile safety. We assumed that many accidents were not intentional but occurred because of poor design or shoddy workmanship by the auto manufacturers, or from human exhaustion, inebriation, anger, bad judgment, or inattention. We had evidence—albeit less than rock solid evidence—that seat belts, air bags, speed limits, wider highway lanes, and enhanced safety design of cars (mounting gasoline tanks so that they are unlikely to explode upon rear impact, introducing anti-lock brakes, etc.) worked. Doubtless some policies failed or were only marginally successful. Others worked stellarly. Over time we assembled an array of rules, laws, and regulations that significantly decreased the number of automobile deaths per mile driven (Insurance Institute for Highway Safety 2016). Pro-control advocates think we can do the same with gun control measures. As a plan to save lives, this is a strategy we should not only consider but pursue. Following are some promising specific proposals. Even if some fail, we need not despair. Some will work. Especially when paired with indirect approaches to gun control that I propose toward the end of the chapter.

SOME FEASIBLE MEASURES

Assault Weapons Bans

There is some dispute about what such bans would cover. Minimally they cover fully automatic weapons (depressing the trigger fires multiple bullets). In many jurisdictions it also covers semi-automatic weapons (the trigger must be squeezed to fire each bullet, but since the spent cartridges are automatically ejected and a new one automatically loaded into the firing chamber, a shooter can average shooting close to one bullet a second). There is no compelling rationale for generally allowing people to have such weapons. Moreover, there are demonstrable costs of permitting them: when they are used in rampage or spree killings (think Virginia Tech, Newtown, and Orlando), the shooter can kill a large number of people in a very short time. It is also easier for a young child bearing such a weapon to kill others accidentally.

Of course, gun advocates will deny the first claim. They insist that there is a compelling rationale for having them: there are occasions where having them could be beneficial for self-defense. I would be shocked where that not sometimes true. Of course it is also true on occasion that having artillery would sometimes be useful for self-defense. Artillery would be close to essential if one were battling a totalitarian regime.

However, even strong gun advocates pooh-pooh the idea that we should allow private ownership of heavy weapons (Hunt, L. H. 2016: 41). They acknowledge that there would be few cases when these would be necessary. They also acknowledge that although the number of people killed with these weapons is relatively small, the risks to others of allowing their private ownership are significant. Therefore, we can legitimately ban them.

We can use the argument they make against permitting the private ownership of bazookas to explain why we may legitimately ban assault weapons. Assault weapons do not have obvious important uses, they are dangerous, and they are not infrequently used to intimidate others, including government officials (Stanglin, D. 2013; Domonoske, C. 2017). There is one additional obvious difference that weighs *against* permitting assault weapons: no one can meander into a school or mall or theater with a bazooka. However, a number of spree killings do involve assault weapons. They are small enough to carry and powerful and fast enough to shoot large numbers of people in a very short time.

Body Armor Ban

We should not permit anyone other than police or the military to have body armor. It is not that there are not situations in which a private citizen might benefit from having it. There are. However, most people assume that such cases would be rare; in contrast, allowing ordinary citizens to purchase such protection would make it easier for criminals to acquire it as well. Police officers would have more trouble stopping criminals wearing a Kevlar vest. Moreover, robbers or potential killers wearing such armor would make it more difficult for ordinary citizens to defend themselves with a handgun. Those who want to be able to defend themselves against criminals with vests would then have reason to obtain Kevlar-penetrating bullets for self-defense. Of course, once *these* became widely available, they, too, would be more easily acquired by criminals. The cycle of escalation this would encourage should worry us.

Waiting Periods

Waiting periods would not prohibit anyone from owning a gun. They would simply ensure that an individual could not purchase one on a whim or an episodic desire for revenge. Individuals would have to apply for a license and then wait a specified length of time before acquiring the weapon. Even a two- or three-day waiting period may give someone time to "cool off." Indeed, a waiting period will likely inhibit some people from going to the trouble of trying to obtain a firearm.

Maintaining and Expanding Gun-Free Zones

Gun-free zones are areas where private citizens cannot carry guns, even if they have a carry permit. We designate an area a gun-free zone if we think admitting armed private citizens there would be too risky for innocent others. We always designate airlines as gun-free zones. Typically we also so designate schools, government buildings, bars, night clubs, and so on. Why? We fear that an armed person in such an environment could kill or maim numerous people if she were mentally unstable, depressed, irate, inebriated, or wanted to make a political statement. Fights regularly break out in bars. If the disputants are armed, one might shoot the other. In a crowded nightclub, mall, or theater once one person starts shooting, others may follow suit, even if in self-defense. Certainly that would happen if we allowed all prison inmates to be armed. If nothing else, this shows that it is not *categorically* true that "more guns, less crime" (McMahan, J. 2016).

The NRA claims these bans are counterproductive since armed citizens could stop a spree or rampage killer. Lott agrees (Lott, J. R., Jr. 2010/2000/1997: 4022). I have no doubt that that could happen. I also have no doubt that gun-free zones have saved many lives, not only from a planned attack but also from potential crossfire of armed citizens trying to down the shooter. One clear bit of evidence that most pro-gun advocates do not believe their own claims about gun-free zones is that the United States House and Senate floors do not allow representatives or visitors to be armed. That is incompatible with the contention of those who control these legislative bodies that gun-free zones are a bad idea. Behavior speaks louder than words.

Repealing Stand Your Ground Statutes

Stand your ground laws "allow individuals to use force, including lethal force, in self-defense when there is reasonable belief of a threat, without having any duty to retreat first" (McClellan, C. B. and Tekin, E. 2012: 3). Such statutes were passed to give people greater latitude when defending their homes or themselves. One of the earliest such laws was passed in Florida. Two different studies found that passage of these laws led to (a) more homicides being deemed "justified" *and* (b) more homicides in the state that adopted the law (Humphreys, D., Gasparrini, A. and Wiebe, D. 2017a; Humphreys, D., Gasparrini, A., and Wiebe, D. 2017b; Hoekstra, M. and Cheng, C. 2013). If this evidence is reliable, and it certainly seems plausible, then these laws are detrimental and should be repealed.

Higher Taxes on Guns

There are two rationales for taxing guns at a higher rate than other consumer items. One, since the widespread availability of guns partly explains gun violence, a tax might slightly lower gun prevalence and, thus, gun violence. A higher tax could make, people who do not really need firearms less inclined to purchase them. Two, a higher tax on guns is fair to those who do not own guns. The public pays more than $700 million a year for uninsured hospital costs for people with gunshot wounds (Spitzer, S. A., Staudenmayer, K. L. et al. 2017). Doubtless, too, we all pay higher medical insurance premiums to defray medical expenses for gunshot victims who do have insurance. To ease this burden on the taxpaying and insurance-paying public, we could specify that all additional tax revenues go toward covering these hospital and insurance costs. I do not expect that these taxes would cover all such costs. However, they would help. This is a straightforward way of asking people who own guns to bear the financial burdens of that ownership.

There is an additional rationale for higher taxes, at least for those who can afford it. If gun advocates are sincere in saying that the core reason for private gun ownership is self-defense, and if they are correct in claiming that the poor bear the principal burden of gun violence, then higher taxes on wealthy owners could underwrite the fees and taxes on guns that the poor must pay for guns they need.

Limiting or Controlling Private Gun Sales and Transfers

Many criminals who obtain weapons get them from a friend or family member, or purchase them privately from someone within their neighborhood (Cook, P. J., Parker, S. T., and Pollack, H. A. 2015: 35). If such transfers were prohibited or had to meet the same registration requirements as purchases of guns from retailers, then this would decrease criminals' access to firearms.

Registration

This is simply one effect of the previous consideration. If all gun purchases had to be registered, then we would have a way to trace the ownership of weapons used in the commission of a crime. More importantly, we need registration to ensure that some people (four-year-olds, certifiably mentally ill people, former violent felons, etc.) are not allowed to acquire guns, and that no one is permitted to purchase some firearms (a working bazooka).

Revoke Immunity for Gun Manufacturers

In 2005 Congress passed the so-called Protection of Lawful Commerce in Arms Act (PLCAA), which gives gun manufacturers and retailers broad legal immunity against suits "result[ing] from the criminal or lawful misuse" of firearms or ammunition (15 USC §§ 7901-7790). Without overwhelming and indisputable evidence of (a) the enormous benefits of private gun ownership and (b) overwhelming and indisputable evidence of a tsunami of baseless and expensive lawsuits against gun manufacturers, it is difficult to imagine any faintly plausible rationale for this law. We have no evidence for either claim.

We do not protect other manufacturers, including those who produce demonstrably valuable goods, for example, automobiles (Henningsen vs. Bloomfield Motors, Inc. 32 N.J. 358, 161 A.2d 69 [1960]). There is no rationale for this exemption. Revoking this law would make gun manufacturers more careful when designing and marketing guns.

Requiring Safer Storage of Guns

We could limit the number of children's suicides, accidental deaths, or deaths caused by children with guns. Likely we would also lower homicides prompted by momentary anger or rage, if we required gun owners to keep their guns stored more securely, for instance, in a gun safe (Miller, M. et al. 2005).

I think all the above measures are prudent. However, rather than simply trying to directly control guns, we should also consider the merits of indirect control.

INDIRECTLY CONTROLLING GUNS

We might make progress if we could move the debate as it is commonly framed into the argumentative background. That debate will not vanish; it raises questions that must eventually be confronted. While waiting for significant breakthroughs from implementing the aforementioned proposals, we would be wise to deploy an indirect strategy for controlling guns that is plausible inasmuch as it is embodied in a number of current and widely acceptable laws, is fair, and should be rationally acceptable to all perspectives on this contentious debate. The approach should achieve many aims of gun control by less coercive means, while still permitting many citizens to own guns.

The attempt to achieve desirable public ends without relying primarily on the force of criminal law is old legal hat. Such efforts would alter the conditions under which citizens make decisions so that they subsequently pursue preferred behaviors.

Of course criminal law also seeks to alter people's behavior by changing the conditions under which they make decisions. By making speeding a crime, the state seeks to make people drive more slowly and more carefully. The criminal law pursues its aims directly by making the undesired behavior illegal; it reinforces these express aims by threatening those who violate the proscribed behavior.

In contrast, indirect measures do not rely primarily on criminal law; often they do not even specify the behavior they want people to pursue or avoid. If these approaches use the criminal law at all, it is by specifying how the state will respond to those who flout the regulation, rule, or policy. Even then, the criminal law is not the primary means of obtaining compliance. Indirect laws standardly *entice* people to pursue beneficial behaviors; they typically dangle monetary carrots rather than wielding penal sticks.

We use this approach in multiple venues. For example, the government wants to encourage home ownership, but it does not require it. Instead, the government instituted policies making home ownership more attractive to prudent citizens: it allowed citizens to deduct home mortgage interest and property taxes from taxable income. These options encourage more people to buy their own homes by providing homebuyers more spendable money.

The government also wants to encourage charitable giving. However, it does not require it. What the government did was to permit citizens to exclude charitable contributions from taxable income. This approach is buttressed by a sizeable inheritance tax on high-value estates (worth more than $10 million) coupled with laws exempting charitable contributions from that portion of an inheritance subject to the estate tax. Both measures increase charitable giving indirectly by making contributions more financially attractive and less financially painful (Blackman, A. 2015).

Other times the government uses blended approaches, employing both direct and indirect means to attain the desired aim. The government wants to lower our carbon footprint. One means of doing that is to get more citizens to purchase more fuel-efficient cars and to drive fewer miles. The government could have chosen to use a criminal hammer to achieve these ends: it could have forbidden drivers from purchasing gas guzzlers or limited the number of miles a citizen can drive each year. It didn't. Instead, it required manufacturers to produce progressively more fuel-efficient autos and provided financial incentives for state and local governments to deploy mass transit systems that diminish citizens' dependence on private autos. It could also provide incentives to encourage citizens to purchase more fuel-efficient models: directly by providing tax breaks for extremely efficient models, and indirectly by placing higher taxes on gasoline. Each element would reinforce the others.

To offer one last example: the state wants citizens to save toward retirement. They use one direct means: they require (most) workers to contribute to Social Security. They also use an indirect means: they established income tax breaks that make additional retirement contributions (explicit retirement plans, 401(K)s, etc.) exempt from income taxes, and therefore, more attractive.

None of these indirect means ensures that everyone acts prudently. Not everyone buys a house. Not everyone gives to charity. Not everyone makes additional retirement savings. However, *enough* people do these actions to make this indirect strategy effective.

I suggest that we employ a blended approach to controlling guns. The ultimate aim of these policies is to lessen the frequency and degree of gun harm (Hemenway, D. 2010/2006). We could somewhat achieve this aim directly by limiting who has access to some guns. Even the United States uses this approach to some degree. In most states violent felons, young children, and the (demonstrably) mentally ill cannot purchase guns (Swanson, J. W. et al. 2015). In no states can private citizens own functional heavy artillery. I see no reason to abandon these minimal direct measures. We can do this without any danger of having Prohibition-like problems. We can also directly specify how people can obtain and store, and whether (and where) they can carry, guns.

We could lessen gun violence indirectly by requiring citizens to have adequate liability insurance on guns they own, by demanding that they take financial responsibility for harm caused by their

ownership of guns. Of course, there is no way to police such a requirement without a robust registration scheme and without having potent
penalties for citizens who refuse to purchase insurance. As I explain
in the following sections, this parallels the common requirement that
automobile drivers have liability insurance. That requirement can be
enforced only if we license and register all autos and drivers.

The aim of the requirement is to alter parameters shaping people's
decisions so that they find beneficial behaviors more attractive and
careless ones less so. It also means then when people are harmed by
firearms, the victims standardly receive (hopefully adequate) compensatory damages and in more serious cases, punitive ones. This
would ensure that gun owners bear the financial responsibility for
harm their owning guns causes.

I begin by explaining what liability insurance is. I argue that prudent gun owners would want such insurance. Finally, I explain when
and why the state can legitimately require them to be insured.

Liability Insurance

WHAT IT IS

We should want to protect ourselves and our fellow citizens from
harm. We have multiple public health measures designed to do just
that. We have laws protecting workers, home owners, consumers,
and patients. When such measures are absent, flawed, or simply
fail (no system is perfect), we want those harmed to be appropriately compensated. Liability insurance is an established method of
assuring that those harmed are compensated for their expenses, pain,
and suffering. Everyone who engages in the activity contributes to
the financial pool from which we compensate those harmed. Since
only a small portion of those engaging in these activities actually
causes harm, this is a reasonably affordable way of appropriately
compensating victims.

WHO PAYS RECOMPENSE?

Barring special considerations, we expect that the person causing harm to pay recompense. The point is simple, familiar, and pervasive in our legal system and our common morality. We praise Joan but not Bruce for her accomplishments. We require Joan, but not Bruce to pay for harms she caused. Assuming Joan has insurance, her insurance carrier pays on her behalf. However, although this is the default, were we to discover in some case that a pressing secondary aim undermines the primary one, then we may explore alternative means to ensure that those harmed are adequately compensated. That is what we do to protect those harmed in automobile accidents. We expect the insurance carrier of the driver at fault to pay the injured person's expenses. Although most US states rely on a fault system of compensatory justice, our system is neither sufficient nor efficient. We face a stubborn reality: far too many drivers are un- or under-insured. Since few people can adequately compensate a victim out of their pockets if they cause others substantial harm, then the core aim of guaranteeing adequate compensation is not satisfied by a pure fault system, at least not the one currently in place in the United States.

That explains why many states now have hybrid systems. Although they rely to a degree on an assignment of fault, they augment this system with mechanisms to guarantee that victims are compensated even when the other driver is neither wealthy nor adequately insured. For instance, in some states drivers are required to have personal injury protection (PIP) to pay their own medical costs after an accident, even if the accident is someone else's fault. That protects them even if other drivers are not properly insured. Insurance companies also encourage drivers to carry excess un- and under-insured motorists' coverage to provide compensation for property damages if the other driver does not or cannot make adequate recompense. Legislators and insurance companies instituted these variations not because the fault system is in principle flawed. Rather they used these measures because the fault system is flawed in practice. These hybrid systems have one overarching aim: to diminish the number of people who are harmed and inadequately compensated.

Despite these supplements to the fault system, no state entirely abandons it. All but one state require all drivers to have liability insurance; the one that does not (New Hampshire) requires that the driver in an accident be able to post a bond equivalent to the minimum required liability coverage (Insurance Information Institute 2016).

In short, despite some variation, our automobile liability system remains steeped in the conviction that those causing harm should compensate for that harm. Insurance is the most common means of paying that compensation (if the costs are more than minimal).

Similar complexities emerged in attempts to guarantee compensation for non-US citizens injured in the conduct of biomedical research. The United States, unlike European countries, has insisted that victims can recoup compensatory medical and personal damages only if they successfully sue in a US court. This requirement makes it effectively impossible for harmed non-US citizens (who are subjects of these experiments) to obtain compensation (Pike, E. R. 2014: 184). In response, ethicists have urged all countries to adopt a no-fault system of compensation whereby researchers would pay recompense even if those harmed cannot *legally* establish that they were harmed by said research (Kamalo, P. D., Manda-Taylor, L., and Rennie, S. 2016). These advocates claim that since biomedical research is intrinsically risky, those who are injured should be compensated, no matter how beneficial the research and no matter how careful and conscientious the researchers. The proposal is morally akin to one I offer in the final section of this paper.

PRUDENT PEOPLE WANT LIABILITY INSURANCE

Prudent and morally sensitive drivers want liability insurance. All drivers should want to be financially capable of meeting her moral responsibility to compensate anyone she harms. However, even if she were indifferent to others' interests, she would want to protect herself from financial ruin if she had to personally pay all costs of harm she wrought. No matter how rigorous our licensing requirements, drivers will sometimes have accidents. They will make perceptual and reasoning errors; they will fail to be appropriately attentive, they will drive while exhausted or ill or depressed or inebriated; sometimes they will just have bad luck. Regardless of the explanation, we know that even careful drivers can cause serious harm to themselves and others.

Of course, sometimes the harm to others is relatively minor, perhaps a few thousand dollars to repair the other driver's automobile. Sometimes the harm is major: the other auto is damaged beyond repair, and either the driver or passenger of the other car has significant medical injuries. In a small percentage of accidents, the damage is calamitous: the driver or passenger of the other car is killed or incurs significant and long-term medical expenses, for example, she becomes permanently disabled.

If that happens and I am at fault, then I must compensate the victim for these expenses. I can be confident that those costs will not come out of my financial hide only if I have adequate liability insurance. Without such insurance, I must be prepared to personally bear the entire cost. If I am not *extraordinarily* wealthy, I could lose my home, car, and savings, as well as a chunk of all future earnings. I will lose money I need to provide for the care and education of my children. That is not something I want to happen. As a prudent driver, I have compelling reasons to obtain sufficient liability insurance. These days, that usually requires not only major auto liability coverage but also an umbrella policy to cover expenses beyond the covered maximum.

WHY WE SHOULD REQUIRE DRIVERS TO HAVE LIABILITY INSURANCE

Of course, not everyone is prudent. In some cases they do not purchase insurance to financially cover harm to themselves or damage to their property. More relevant to the current inquiry, many do not voluntarily purchase liability insurance to compensate those they harm. Other people purchase demonstrably insufficient liability insurance. Given that, we have both paternalistic and other-directed reasons to require motorists to have liability insurance. The laws are paternalistic inasmuch as they protect drivers from financial catastrophe if they must pay significant compensation. They are other-directed inasmuch as they protect those harmed by non-wealthy drivers. It also protects third parties from having to compensate victims (through higher taxes or insurance premiums) for harms caused by un- or underinsured drivers. The best way to make things roughly fair is to require all drivers to have liability insurance. I think they should be required to have sufficient coverage to appropriately compensate those they harm.

Mandatory insurance would place a larger financial burden where it should be placed: on those who (1) have more cars, (2) have vehicles more likely to cause more harm, (3) drive more miles, (4) drive in more dangerous environments, and (5) for other reasons (e.g., age) are statistically more likely to cause accidents. These people must pay higher premiums and thus carry a larger percentage of the financial burden. That is as it should be. It would be palpably unfair to expect victims and prudent drivers to carry the financial costs of those who are less prudent and less careful. By requiring liability insurance, we use market mechanisms to discourage drivers from being careless and making imprudent decisions, and we encourage them to be more careful and make more prudent decisions. Unfortunately, we know that is insufficient to adequately protect all drivers since some people are neither careful nor prudent. However, a properly designed mandatory auto insurance program will motivate a substantial number of people to both be more careful and to have adequate insurance to cover feasible monetary claims against them.

We think it is reasonable for states to mandate that drivers—and others who engage in risky activities—have liability insurance. We could, of course, not require insurance but simply insist that offending drivers make appropriate recompense, no matter how much it devastates them or *their* families. This approach would be unsatisfactory for drivers who must shoulder the entire compensation, even though it devastates their families. It would be unsatisfactory for clients since some number of them will be uncompensated or undercompensated. The rationale for expecting drivers to have adequate liability insurance is clear, compelling, and fair. We can apply the same rationale to private gun ownership.

APPLICABILITY TO GUNS

Gun advocates claim guns save lives and prevent harm. Doubtless they sometimes do. Guns, like autos, have benefits. However, even if the benefits of the private ownership of guns were as substantial as advocates claim—and, as we saw in the last chapter that is unlikely—their benefits could not remotely approach those of automobiles. Our society depends upon private transportation. No plausible story makes guns nearly as beneficial. Moreover, private ownership of guns is also a source of harm (Cook, P. J. and Ludwig, J. 2002; Hemenway, D. 2010/2006).

Even people who advocate a serious claim to bear arms, should want to (a) ensure that harmed people are adequately compensated, (b) protect themselves from financial ruin if they are successfully sued for harm caused by their guns, (c) seek ways to lessen the cost of guaranteeing that (a) and (b) are satisfied, (d) discourage people from obtaining guns for trivial or nefarious reasons, and (e) encourage people to be more careful and diligent with firearms they own. Mandating liability insurance for gun owners fulfills all five ends.

I assume we all agree people should be adequately compensated when they are harmed by other people's activities, including owning guns. I also assume that as long as we have the tort system, prudent people want to be protected from having to bear the full burden of compensating someone they harm. Even the NRA claims that purchasing gun liability insurance is prudent. They urge their members to purchase it; they provide links on their website to companies that write gun liability policies (2016). Beginning in 2017, the association expressly endorsed one insurance carrier (Valentine, M. 2017). This idea is not a fiction concocted by pro-control advocates.

Of course, if insurance is the best mechanism for ensuring that (a) and (b) are satisfied, gun owners will want to obtain insurance at the lowest rate for the most robust coverage. Here is where the free market steps in. Auto and home insurance companies standardly offer lower premiums to drivers who take steps to decrease the likelihood that others will be harmed by their clients. Knowing that, prudent home and auto owners pursue ways of lowering their premiums. Auto insurance companies give lower premiums to teenagers who take driver's education. They assume that trained drivers are less likely than untrained ones to have accidents. Homeowners' insurance companies offer reduced premiums to clients who take steps to make their homes less inviting or vulnerable to theft or fire or water damage, for example, by installing deadbolts and security systems, having fire alarms and fire extinguishers, or having an elaborate water drainage system.

Gun insurance companies would do the same. They would offer lower premiums to gun owners who take steps to decrease the chance that they must file a claim. These steps might include passing rigorous gun-safety training, purchasing fewer guns, purchasing guns deemed to be less dangerous, purchasing guns with safety locks or fingerprint-activated triggers. I am not sure what would be included or how large these reductions in premiums would be. Nor do I know how high the premiums would need to be to make writing policies financially feasible.

However, that is not a problem since I think that neither I nor the state should decide these things. Gun insurance companies should. They will carefully analyze data to determine just how dangerous owning guns is; then they will determine how potential safety measures might decrease the probability and severity of a gun owner's causing harm, and thus, of some third party making a successful claim against them. Insurance companies want to avoid paying more and more sizeable claims. Since attenuating harm to others will diminish the size and frequency of claims, then the company wants to encourage owners to act in ways that diminish the chance that others are harmed by their owning firearms.

Insurance companies could establish some firm requirements for gun owners in the way that auto and homeowners insurance companies do. For instance, many home insurers and mortgage companies require home owners to remove dead trees that might fall onto a neighbor's house. They may mandate that homeowners install handrails on steps or high porches to lessen the chance that visitors will fall and hurt themselves. In the same way, gun insurance companies might deem some actions essential for anyone wanting coverage. Which ones? That should be decided by the companies in the free market, based on actuarial judgments about the cost of likelihood of civil complaints against those they cover.

The fourth advantage may not be one that is immediately apparent to gun advocates. But an advantage it is. If gun owners must have coverage, and the company sets the amount of the premium based on their judgment of risk, some high-risk people may be disinclined to purchase guns for insignificant or malicious reasons. If these people do not purchase guns, then the cost of financial awards that must be paid from the insurance pool will decrease. If the size of the payouts decreases, the cost of the premiums should also decrease.

Fifth, it should make prudent gun owners more careful for the same reasons liability insurance makes many drivers more careful. Will this scheme guarantee that only prudent people purchase guns and those that do will act more prudently? Of course not. We know that some insured automobile drivers are reckless. However, the fault system, supported by mandatory auto insurance, encourages enough of them to take more care. We have equally good reason to think a not insignificant number of gun owners would do the same. Indeed, we have one reason to think they might be more likely to either rethink their decision to obtain a weapon or take the necessary steps to lower their premiums. Whereas virtually no one can do without a car or a home, people *can* do without a gun.

There are two related knock-on benefits of this scheme.

One, requiring gun owners to have liability insurance will help create an environment where gun owners are regularly expected to compensate for harm their gun-owning activity causes. This is an environment in which people will be more thoughtful before purchasing a gun and more careful with guns they do purchase. Additionally, juries will be willing to make substantial awards against gun owners when that is warranted.

Two, the state can ascertain that people have the requisite insurance only if they institute a registration program akin to that for automobiles. People would have to register every gun (as they have to register every car) whenever and however they acquire it. In addition to the aforementioned myriad benefits of registration, if someone uses a weapon when committing a crime, it will be easier to identify the owner. Moreover, gun owners will be more careful when selling their weapons to make sure that the purchaser has the requisite license and insurance. These efforts will not end violence, but they should lessen it.

Strict Liability and Insurance

Owning guns is an inherently dangerous activity. Gun owners know that. If they thought owning guns was no more dangerous than owning knives, baseball bats, and crowbars, then they should be happy as long as the state permitted them to defend themselves with these other weapons. They would be proposing shall-issue knife laws and shall-issue crowbar laws and shall-issue baseball bat laws, at least as often as they propose shall-issue handguns laws. They do no such thing. Why? Because they know full well that owning guns is dangerous in a way that owning these other objects is not. That is precisely why they are so keen that people be legally permitted to keep them in their homes and carry them on their persons (Hall, T. 2006: 304). They want to have ready availability to these especially lethal weapons.

Once they acknowledge that owning them is inherently dangerous, they should willingly accept the responsibility for any harm caused by their firearms. As I just argued, liability insurance would be a first, and likely the most important, step. However, we could augment that approach with the legal mechanism of strict liability. It is appropriate for gun ownership just as it is appropriate for dynamite ownership. Dynamite has many beneficial uses. It is essential for our modern economy. However, we know that owning it is an inherently dangerous activity, so we heavily restrict its purchase, storage, and use. I cannot own dynamite for recreation (I like the flash and the noise), for fishing (I am too lazy to drop in a pole or cast a fly), or for protection (I set up tripwires detonating dynamite on my property's perimeter). Despite its enormous value to society, when we permit people to own it, we subject them to strict legal liability. An owner is financially liable for harm caused by his dynamite, even if he were not negligent.

For similar reasons, I propose that we make handgun owners (and perhaps ultimately all gun owners) strictly liable for harm caused by the use of their guns. If Jones's child takes his gun and kills someone while committing a crime, then Jones will be financially responsible to those harmed. If Jones's child accidentally kills a neighbor's child, Jones will be financially responsible to the other child's family. Indeed, I suspect this is probably already common practice in many jurisdictions. Making gun ownership strictly liable would legally codify that practice.

Given the nature of tort law, it may well be that if someone steals Jones's gun and kills someone with it, then Jones could be successfully sued in some jurisdictions. If Jones were negligent in storing his gun, he would probably be required to pay punitive damages. If he were grossly negligent (he left it lying in his front yard, next to a school playground), we might even bring criminal charges against him (reckless endangerment).

Lester Hunt would object since he does not think that owning guns is inherently dangerous. If used properly, he claims, owning guns is *completely* safe; others are in no danger (Hunt, L. H. 2016: 71-72). Hunt's claim is false or trivially true. It is true only if Hunt builds into the definition of "proper use" the requirement that no innocent person be harmed. So defined, the claim would be true . . . but irrelevant to this debate. What matters is what happens when large swaths of citizens own guns. In this world, innocent people are harmed by guns. A lot of them. Additionally, if he really thought that no harm could come from people owning guns, then he should not object to the use of strict liability. Since no one would ever be harmed by people's owning guns, then no one would ever be held strictly liable. No harm, no foul. The law might be useless but it would not be inappropriate.

Since innocent people are not infrequently hurt by guns, it is only fair to expect people to take responsibility for harm that arises from their inherently risky actions. Having strict liability, in tandem with mandatory liability insurance, will make some people who do not need guns less inclined to obtain them, while a sufficient number who choose to have guns will take more care in storing, handling, using, and transferring them. This mechanism would arguably achieve the central aims of gun control without making gun ownership against the law. It is preferable to the current scheme where guns are easily obtainable in the United States and where a majority of those who are harmed by firearms are uncompensated, or if they are compensated, the money comes from public coffers.

My proposal for mandatory liability insurance would augment a policy of strict liability without financially crippling gun users. That's not quite right. If the free market decided that the danger of underwriting gun ownership were financially infeasible, or if they can offer coverage only at exorbitant rates, then that would limit the number of people who can actually own guns. However, were that true, we would be confident that the dangers of allowing gun ownership were excessive. In contrast, were guns as safe as Hunt avers, insurance companies would pounce on the possibility of writing lucrative policies. Policies would be widely available; premiums, astonishingly cheap. On the other hand, were Hunt mistaken, premiums would be high. However, this does not count against the proposal since the companies would determine cost based on their objective assessment of the risk of privately owning guns.

Perhaps these indirect mechanisms will not work. However, it is plausible to think they, coupled with the more concrete proposals advocated in the previous major section, would have the benefits of gun control without depriving most people of the ability to own firearms for self-defense. These mechanisms are a form of serious gun control that guns owners should willingly accept.

BIBLIOGRAPHY

Almasy, S. (2014) "Dad's Texting to Daughter Sparks Argument, Fatal Shooting in Movie Theater." CNN. [Online] Available at: http://www.cnn.com/2014/01/13/justice/florida-movie-theater-shooting/. [Accessed: 23 November 2016].

American Psychological Association (2011) "Amicus Brief in Commonwealth of Pennsylvania vs. Benjamin Walker." [Online] Available at: http://www.apa.org/about/offices/ogc/amicus/walker.pdf. [Accessed: 3 September 2013].

Amy, D. (2007) "Government Is Good: An Unapologetic Defense of a Vital Institution." [Online] Available at: http://www.governmentisgood.com/. [Accessed: 22 October 2016].

Appiah, K. A. (2011) "'Group Rights' and Racial Affirmative Action." *Journal of Ethics* **15** (3), 265–280.

Ayres, I., and Donohue, J. J., III (2003) "Shooting Down the 'More Guns, Less Crime' Hypothesis." *Stanford Law Review* **55** (4), 1193–1312.

Bar-Ilan, J., Keenoy, K., Levene, M., and Yaari, E. (2009) "Presentation Bias Is Significant in Determining User Preference for Search Results—a User Study." *Journal of the American Society for Information Science and Technology* **60** (1), 135–149.

Beitz, C. R. (2009) *The Idea of Human Rights.* Oxford: Oxford University Press.

Blackman, A. (2015) "The Surprising Relationship between Taxes and Charitable Giving." *Wall Street Journal,* 12 December. [Online] Available at: https://www.wsj.com/articles/the-surprising-relationship-between-taxes-and-charitable-giving-1450062191. [Accessed: 20 May 2016].

Brighouse, H. (2006) *On Education.* London: Routledge.

Buchanan, A. (2013) *The Heart of Human Rights.* New York: Oxford University Press.

Buchanan, B. J. (2006) *Gunpowder, Explosives and the State: A Technological History.* Farnham, UK: Ashgate Publishing, Ltd.

—— (1996) *Gunpowder: The History of an International Technology.* Bath, UK: Bath University Press.

Buckley, W. F., Jr. (2002/1996) "The War on Drugs Is Lost." In LaFollette, H. (ed.) *Ethics in Practice.* 2nd ed. Oxford: Blackwell: 300–306.

Bureau of Justice Statistics (2017) "National Crime Victimization Survey." Washington, DC: Government Printing Office. [Online] Available at: https://www.bjs.gov/index.cfm?ty=dcdetail&iid=245. [Accessed: 12 August 2017].

Burton, R. A. (2009) *On Being Certain: Believing You Are Right Even When You're Not.* New York: St. Martin's.

Cassino, D. (2013) "Beliefs about Sandy Hook Cover-up, Coming Revolution Underlie Divide on Gun Control." [Online] Available at: http://www.huffingtonpost.com/2013/05/02/poll-armed-revolution_n_3203315.html. [Accessed: 5 September 2017].

Centers for Disease Control and Prevention (2016) "Health Statistics: Measuring Our Nation's Health." [Online] Available at: http://www.cdc.gov/nchs/data/factsheets/factsheet_health_statistics.htm. [Accessed: 8 August 2017].

—— (1997) "Monthly Vital Statistics Report." 45 Atlanta, GA: Centers for Disease Control and Prevention.

Chase, K. (2003) *Firearms: A Global History to 1700.* Cambridge: Cambridge University Press.

Childress, J. F. (1980) "Negative and Positive Rights." *Hastings Center Report* **10** (1), 19.

CNN (2016) "Michigan Shooting: Inmate Kills 2 Bailiffs, Sheriff Says." *CNN* [Online] Available at: http://www.cnn.com/2016/07/11/us/michigan-courthouse-shooting/index.html. [Accessed: 12 July 2016].

Cook, P. and Ludwig, J. (1996) "Guns in America: Results of a Comprehensive National Survey on Firearms Ownership and Use." Washington, DC: Police Foundation.

Cook, P. J. (2013) "The Great American Gun War: Notes from Four Decades in the Trenches." *Crime and Justice* **42** (1), 19–73.

Cook, P. J. and Ludwig, J. (2002) *Gun Violence: The Real Cost.* Oxford: Oxford University Press.

—— (1996) "You Got Me: How Many Defensive Gun Uses per Year?" American Society of Criminology, Chicago.

Cook, P. J., Parker, S. T., and Pollack, H. A. (2015) "Sources of Guns to Dangerous People: What We Learn by Asking Them." *Preventive Medicine* **79**, 28–36.

DeGrazia, D. (2016) "The Case For." In DeGrazia, D. and Hunt, L. H. (eds.) *Debating Gun Control: How Much Regulation Do We Need?* Kindle ed. New York: Oxford University Press: 1645–3486.

Deloria, V., Jr. (1969) *Custer Died for Your Sins: An Indian Manifesto.* Norman: Oklahoma University Press.

Domonoske, C. (2017) "1st Trial over Nevada Standoff Begins for Cliven Bundy Followers." *National Public Radio,* 6 February 2017. [Online] Available at: http://www.npr.org/sections/thetwo-way/2017/02/06/513702096/1st-trial-over-nevada-standoff-begins-for-cliven-bundy-followers. [Accessed: 19 August 2017].

Dunning, D. (2005) *Self-Insight: Roadblocks and Detours on the Path to Knowing Thyself.* New York: Psychology Press.

Dunning, D., Heath, C., and Suls, J. M. (2005) "Flawed Self-Assessment: Implications for Health, Education, and the Workplace." *Psychological Science in the Public Interest* **5** (3), 69–106.

Dworkin, R. M. (1977) *Taking Rights Seriously.* Cambridge, MA: Harvard University Press.

Ehrlinger, J., Gilovich, T., and Ross, L. (2005) "Peering into the Bias Blind Spot: People's Assessments of Bias in Themselves and Others." *Personality and Social Psychology Bulletin* **31** (5), 1–13.

Ellis, L. and Walsh, A. (2003) "Crime, Delinquency and Intelligence: A Review of the Worldwide Literature." In Nyborg, H. (ed.) *The Scientific Study of General Intelligence: Tribute to Arthur R. Jenson.* New York: Pergamon Press:342–366.

Erdman, J. (2015) "In Flash Flooding, Your Vehicle Can Be Biggest Danger." [Online] Available at: https://weather.com/safety/floods/news/flash-flooding-vehicle-danger-20140717. [Accessed: 1 September 2017].

Federal Bureau of Investigation (2017) "Crime in the United States 2015." Washington, DC: US Department of Justice. [Online] Available at: https://ucr.fbi.gov/crime-in-the-u.s/2015/crime-in-the-u.s.-2015. [Accessed: 13 August 2017].

—— (2016) "Uniform Reporting Crime Handbook." Washington, DC: US Department of Justice. [Online] Available at: https://ucr.fbi.gov/additional-ucr-publications/ucr_handbook.pdf/at_download/file. [Accessed: 29 December 2017].

Feinberg, J. (1988) *Harmless Wrongdoing.* New York: Oxford University Press.

—— (1986) *Harm to Self.* New York: Oxford University Press.

—— (1985) *Offense to Others.* New York: Oxford University Press.

—— (1984) *Harm to Others.* New York: Oxford University Press.

—— (1970) "The Nature and Value of Rights." *Journal of Value Inquiry* **4** (4), 243–260.

—— (1966) "Duties, Rights, and Claims." *American Philosophical Quarterly* **3** (2), 137–144.

Festinger, L. (1957) *A Theory of Cognitive Dissonance.* Stanford, CA: Stanford University Press.

Fields, G. and McWhirter, C. (2012) "In Medical Triumph, Homicides Fall Despite Soaring Gun Violence." *Wall Street Journal,* 8 December. [Online] Available at: http://online.wsj.com/article/SB10001424127887324712504578131360 684277812.html. [Accessed: 18 December 2016].

Final Conference on the Arms Trade Treaty (2013) "Draft Decision." New York: United Nations. [Online] Available at: http://www.un.org/disarmament/ATT/docs/Draft_ATT_text_27_Mar_2013-E.pdf. [Accessed: 20 July 2013].

Framingham Heart Study (2016) "Framingham Heart Study." [Online] Available at: https://www.framinghamheartstudy.org/. [Accessed: 11 September 2013].

Freedman, D. A. (2010) *Statistical Models and Causal Inference: A Dialogue with the Social Sciences.* Kindle ed. Cambridge: Cambridge University Press.

Fulton, S. and Martin, T. (2017) *Rest in Power: The Enduring Life of Trayvon Martin.* 1st ed. New York: Spiegel & Grau.

General Social Survey (2015) "Trends in Gun Ownership in the United States, 1974–2014." NORC at the University of Chicago. [Online] Available at: http:// www.norc.org/PDFs/GSS%20Reports/GSS_Trends%20in%20Gun%20 Ownership_US_1972-2014.pdf. [Accessed: 29 May 2015].

Gewirth, A. (2001) "Are All Rights Positive?" *Philosophy and Public Affairs* **30** (3), 321–333.

Glendon, M. A. (1993) *Rights Talk: The Impoverishment of Political Discourse.* New York: Free Press.

Griffin, J. (2008) *On Human Rights.* Oxford: Oxford University Press.

Grinshteyn, E. and Hemenway, D. (2016) "Violent Death Rates: The US Compared with Other High-Income OECD Countries, 2010." *American Journal of Medicine* **129** (3), 266–273.

Haag, P. (2016) *The Gunning of America: Business and the Making of American Gun Culture.* New York: Basic Books.

Hall, T. (2006) "Is There a Right to Bear Arms?" *Public Affairs Quarterly* **20** (4), 293–312.

Hansford, B. C. and Hattie, J. A. (1982) "The Relationship between Self and Achievement/Performance Measures." *Review of Educational Research* **52** (1), 123–142.

Harvard University Library Open Collections (2017) "Germ Theory." *Contagion: Historical Views of Diseases and Epidemics.* [Online] Available at: http://ocp.hul. harvard.edu/contagion/germtheory.html. [Accessed: 23 August 2017].

Hemenway, D. (2010/2006) *Private Guns, Public Health.* Kindle ed. Ann Arbor: University of Michigan Press.

—— (1997a) "The Myth of Millions of Annual Self-Defense Gun Uses: A Case Study of Survey Overestimates of Rare Events." *Chance* **10** (3), 6–10.

—— (1997b) "Survey Research and Self-Defense Gun Use: An Explanation of Extreme Overestimates." *Journal of Criminal Law and Criminology* **87** (4), 1430–145.

Hemenway, D. and Nolan, E. P. (2017) "The Scientific Agreement on Firearm Issues." *Injury Prevention* **23** (4), 221–225.

Hempel, C. G. (1966) *Philosophy of Natural Science.* Englewood Cliffs, NJ: Prentice-Hall.

Hennessy-Fiske, M. and Banerjee, N. (2011) "Armed Bystander's Reaction in Ariz. Shootings Illustrates Complexity of Gun Debate." *Denver Post.* [Online] Available at: http://www.denverpost.com/nationworld/ci_17109372. [Accessed: 1 May 2013].

Hepburn, L. M. and Hemenway, D. (2004) "Firearm Availability and Homicide: A Review of the Literature." *Aggression and Violent Behavior* **9** (4), 417–440.

Hoekstra, M. and Cheng, C. (2013) "Does Strengthening Self-Defense Law Deter Crime or Escalate Violence? Evidence from Expansion to Castle Doctrine." *Journal of Human Resources* **48** (3), 821–854.

Holmes, S. and Sunstein, C. R. (2000) *The Cost of Rights: Why Liberty Depends on Taxes.* New York: W. W. Norton.

Horowitz, J. L. (2004) "Statistical Issues in the Evaluation of the Effects of Right-to-Carry Laws." In Wellford, C. F., Pepper, J. V. and Petrie, C. V. (eds.) *Firearms and Violence: A Critical Review.* New York: National Academy Press:299–308. [Online] Available at: http://www.nap.edu/catalog/10881.html. [Accessed: 8 September 2013].

Huemer, M. (2003) "Is There a Right to Own a Gun?" *Social Theory and Practice* **29** (2), 297–324.

Humphreys, D., Gasparrini, A., and Wiebe, D. J. (2017a) "Evaluating the Impact of Florida's 'Stand Your Ground' Self-Defense Law on Homicide and Suicide by Firearm: An Interrupted Time Series Study." *JAMA Internal Medicine* **177** (1), 44–50.

——— (2017b) "Association between Enactment of a 'Stand Your Ground' Self-Defense Law and Unlawful Homicides in Florida." *JAMA Internal Medicine* **177** (10), 1523–1524.

Huff, D. (1993/1954) *How to Lie with Statistics.* New York: W. W. Norton.

Hunt, L. H. (2016) "The Case Against." In DeGrazia, D. and Hunt, L. H. (eds.) *Debating Gun Control: How Much Regulation Do We Need?* Kindle ed. New York: Oxford University Press:138–1628.

——— (2011) "The Right to Arms as a Means Right." *Public Affairs Quarterly* **25** (2), 113–129.

Husak, D. (2008) *Overcriminalization: The Limits of the Criminal Law.* New York: Oxford University Press.

Insurance Information Institute (2016) "Compulsory Auto/Uninsured Motorists." [Online] Available at: http://www.iii.org/issue-update/compulsory-auto-uninsured-motorists. [Accessed: 28 May 2016].

Insurance Institute for Highway Safety (2016) "Yearly Snapshot." [Online] Available at: http://www.iihs.org/iihs/topics/t/general-statistics/fatalityfacts/over-view-of-fatality-facts. [Accessed: 31 August 2017].

────── (2015) "Improved Vehicle Design Brings Down Death Rates." *Status Report*, 29 January 2015. [Online] Available at: http://www.iihs.org/iihs/sr/statusreport/article/50/1/1. [Accessed: 21 September 2016].

Kahneman, D. (2011) *Thinking, Fast and Slow*. New York: Macmillan.

Kamalo, P. D., Manda-Taylor, L., and Rennie, S. (2016) "Appropriateness of No-Fault Compensation for Research-Related Injuries from an African Perspective: An Appeal for Action by African Countries." *Journal of Medical Ethics* 42, 528–533.

Kant, I. (1991/1785) *The Metaphysics of Morals*. Cambridge: Cambridge University Press.

Kegler, S. R., Baldwin, G. T., Rudd, R. A., and Ballesteros, M. F. (2017) "Increases in United States Life Expectancy through Reductions in Injury-Related Death." *Population Health Metrics* 15 (1), 32. [Online] Available at: https://doi.org/10.1186/s12963-017-0150-4. [Accessed: 4 April 2017].

Kellermann, A. and Rivera, F. (2013) "Silencing the Science on Gun Research." *JAMA* 309 (6), 549–550.

Khazan, O. (2017) "Nearly Half of All Murdered Women Are Killed by Romantic Partners." *The Atlantic*.

Kis, J. (2013) "Berlin's Two Concepts of Positive Liberty." *European Journal of Political Theory* 12 (1), 31–48.

Kleck, G. (1997/2006) *Targeting Guns: Firearms and Their Control*. New York: Aldine De Gruyter.

────── (1991) *Point Blank: Guns and Violence in America*. New Brunswick, NJ: Aldine Transaction.

Kleck, G. and Gertz, M. (1995) "Armed Resistance to Crime: The Prevalence and Nature of Self-Defense with a Gun." *Journal of Criminal Law & Criminology* 86 (1), 150–187.

Kolar, D. W., Funder, D. C., and Colvin, C. R. (1996) "Comparing the Accuracy of Personality Judgments by the Self and Knowledgeable Others." *Journal of Personality* 64 (2), 311–337.

Kopel, D. B. (1992) *The Samurai, the Mountie and the Cowboy*. Buffalo, NY: Prometheus Books.

Kuhn, T. (1962) *The Structure of Scientific Revolutions*. Chicago: University of Chicago Press.

Kyle, C. and Doyle, W. (2013) *American Gun: A History of the U.S. in Ten Firearms*. Kindle ed. New York: William Morrow.

Kymlicka, W. (2001) *Contemporary Political Philosophy: An Introduction*. New York: Oxford University Press.

LaFollette, H. (2017) "The Greatest Vice?" *Journal of Practical Ethics* 4 (2), 1–24.

────── (2005) "Collateral Consequences of Punishment: Civil Penalties Accompanying Formal Punishment." *Journal of Applied Philosophy* 22 (3), 241–261.

—— (2001) "Controlling Guns." *Criminal Justice Ethics* **20** (1), 34–39.

—— (1979) "Why Libertarianism Is Mistaken." In Arthur, J. and Shaw, W. H. (eds.) *Justice and Economic Distribution*. Englewood Cliffs, NJ: Prentice-Hall:194–206.

LaPierre, W. (2013) "Stand and Fight." *The Daily Caller*. [Online] Available at: http://dailycaller.com/2013/02/13/stand-and-fight/. [Accessed: 15 February 2013].

Lippke, R. L. (1995) "The Elusive Distinction between Negative and Positive Rights." *Southern Journal of Philosophy* **33** (3), 335–346.

Locke, J. (1690) *Two Treatises on Civil Government*.

Lott, John R., Jr. (2010/2000/1997) *More Guns, Less Crime: Understanding Crime and Gun-Control Laws*. Kindle, 3rd ed. Chicago: University of Chicago Press.

—— and Mustard, David B. (1997) "Crime, Deterrence, and Right-to-Carry Concealed Handguns." *Journal of Legal Studies* **26** (1), 1–68.

Martin, R. (2013) "Rights." In LaFollette, H. (ed.) *International Encyclopedia of Ethics*. Malden, MA: Wiley Blackwell:4616–4631.

McClellan, C. B. and Tekin, E. (2012) "Stand Your Ground Laws, Homicides, and Injuries." NBER Working Papers Series. Cambridge, MA: National Bureau of Economic Research.

McKeown, T. (1976) *The Modern Rise of Populations*. New York: Academic Press.

McMahan, J. (2016) "A Challenge to Gun Rights." In *Philosophers Take on the World*. Oxford: Oxford University Press:17–20.

—— (2013) "Moral Intuition." In LaFollette, H. and Persson, I. (eds.) *The Blackwell Guide to Ethical Theory*. 2nd ed. Oxford: Blackwell:103–122.

Michaels, D. (2008) *Doubt Is Their Product: How Industry's Assault on Science Threatens Your Health*. New York: Oxford University Press.

Michel, L. and Herbeck, D. (2002) *American Terrorist: Timothy McVeigh & the Tragedy at Oklahoma City*. New York: Avon Books.

Michelson, A. A. and Morley, E. W. (1887) "On the Relative Motion of the Earth and the Luminiferous Ether." *American Journal of Science* **34** (203), 333.

Mill, J. S. (1985/1885) *On Liberty*. Indianapolis, IN: Hackett.

Miller, M., Azrael, D., and Hemenway, D. (2013) "Firearms and Violent Death in the United States." In Webster, D. W. and Vernick, J. S. (eds.) *Reducing Gun Violence in American*. Kindle ed. Baltimore: Johns Hopkins University Press:359–683.

—— (2002a) "Household Firearm Ownership and Suicide Rates in the United States." *Epidemiology* **13** (5), 517–524.

—— (2002b) "Rates of Household Firearm Ownership and Homicide across US Regions and States, 1988-1997." *American Journal of Public Health* **92** (12), 1988–1993.

—— (2000) "Community Firearms, Community Fear." *Epidemiology* **10** (6), 709–714.

—— and Vriniotis, M. (2005) "Firearm Storage Practices and Rates of Unintentional Firearm Deaths in the United States." *Accident Analysis & Prevention* **37** (4), 661–667.

Miller, M. and Hemenway, D. (2008) "Guns and Suicide in the United States." *New England Journal of Medicine* **359** (10), 989–991.

—— (1999) "The Relationship between Firearms and Suicide: A Review of the Literature." *Aggression and Violent Behavior* **4** (1), 59–75.

Nagel, T. (2013) "Forward." In *Anarchy, State, and Utopia.* Kindle ed. New York: Basic Books.

National Rifle Association (2016) "Let Us Help You Get the Protection You Need." [Online] Available at: https://mynrainsurance.com/home. [Accessed: 18 May 2016].

Needham, J. (1985) *Gunpowder as the Fourth Power, East and West: First East Asian History of Science Foundation Lecture, Presented at the University of Hong Kong, 20 October 1983.* Hong Kong: Hong Kong University Press.

Nickel, J. W. (2007) *Making Sense of Human Rights.* 2nd ed. Oxford: Blackwell.

Nickerson, R. S. (1998) "Confirmation Bias: A Ubiquitous Phenomenon in Many Guises." *Review of General Psychology* **2** (2), 175–220.

Northrup, E. (1957) *Science Looks at Smoking: A New Inquiry into the Effects of Smoking.* New York: Coward McCann.

Nozick, R. (2013/1974) *Anarchy, State, and Utopia.* Kindle ed. New York: Basic Books.

Nuland, S. (2004) *The Doctor's Plague: Germs, Childbed Fever, and the Strange Story of Ignaz Semmelweiss.* New York: W. W. Norton.

Oreskes, N. and Conway, E. M. (2010) *Merchants of Doubt: How a Handful of Scientists Obscured the Truth on Issues from Tobacco Smoke to Global Warming.* New York: Bloomsbury.

Pike, E. R. (2014) "In Need of Remedy: US Policy for Compensating Injured Research Participants." *Journal of Medical Ethics* **40** (3), 182–185.

ProCon.org (2014) "35 FDA-Approved Prescription Drugs Later Pulled from the Market." [Online] Available at: http://prescriptiondrugs.procon.org/view.resource.php?resourceID=005528. [Accessed: 9 September 2016].

Pronin, E. (2009) "The Introspection Illusion." *Advances in Experimental Social Psychology* **41**, 1–67.

—— and Kugler, M. B. (2007) "Valuing Thoughts, Ignoring Behavior: The Introspection Illusion as a Source of the Bias Blind Spot." *Journal of Experimental Social Psychology* **43** (4), 565–578.

Pronin, E., Lin, D. Y., and Ross, L. (2002) "The Bias Blind Spot: Perceptions of Bias in Self Versus Others." *Personality and Social Psychology Bulletin* **28** (3), 369.

Rainbolt, G. W. (2014) "Rights." In LaFollette, H. (ed.) *Ethics in Practice.* 4th ed. Malden, MA: Wiley Blackwell:49–59.

—— (2006) *The Concept of Rights.* Dordrecht: Springer.

Raz, J. (2010) "Human Rights without Foundations." In Tasioulas, J. and Besson, S. (eds.) *The Philosophy of International Law.* Oxford: Oxford University Press: 321–331.

—— (1986) *The Morality of Freedom.* Oxford: Clarendon Press.

Rosenfeld, S. (2011) *Common Sense: A Political History.* Cambridge, MA: Harvard University Press.

Sacks, O. (2013) "Speak, Memory." *New York Review of Books* **60** (3), 19–22.

Scheffler, S. (1992) *Human Morality.* Oxford: Oxford University Press.

Seigenthaler, J., Squires, J., Hemphill, P., and Ritter, F. (1971) *Search for Justice.* Nashville, TN: Aurora.

Shue, H. (1996/1980) *Basic Rights: Subsistence, Affluence, and U.S. Foreign Policy.* 2nd ed. Princeton, NJ: Princeton University Press.

Sinnott-Armstrong, W. (2008) "Framing Moral Intuitions." In Sinnott-Armstrong, W. (ed.) *Moral Psychology: The Cognitive Science of Morality.* Kindle ed. Cambridge, MA: MIT Press:743–1163.

Snyder, T. (2010) *Bloodlands: Europe Beween Hitler and Stalin.* New York: Basic Books.

Spitzer, S. A., Staudenmayer, K. L., Tennakoon, L., Spain, D. A., and Weiser, T. G. (2017) "Costs and Financial Burden of Initial Hospitalizations for Firearm Injuries in the United States, 2006–2014." *American Journal of Public Health* **107** (5), 770–774.

Stanglin, D. (2013) "Armed Protesters Rattle Texas Mom's Gun-Control Meeting." *USA Today,* 11 November. [Online] Available at: https://www.usatoday.com/story/news/nation/2013/11/11/moms-demand-action-open-carry-texas-guns-rifles/3497895/. [Accessed: 25 November 2013].

Stell, L. (2001) "Gun Control and the Regulation of Fundamental Rights." *Criminal Justice Ethics* **20** (1), 28–33.

Stevenson, K. (2013) "1800–1900: Changes in Urban/Rural U.S. Population." Elderweb. [Online] Available at: https://www.elderweb.com/book/appendix/1800-1990-changes-urbanrural-us-population/. [Accessed: 15 January 2016].

Sumner, L. W. (1987) *The Moral Foundation of Rights.* Oxford: Oxford University Press.

Swanson, J. W. and Robertson, A. G. (2013) "Thinking Differently About Mental Illness, Violence Risk, and Gun Rights." In Webster, D. W., and Vernick, J. S. (eds.) *Updated Evidence and Policy Developments on Reducing Gun Violence in America.* Baltimore: Johns Hopkins University Press.

Swanson, J. W., Sampson, N. A., Petukhova, M. V., Zaslavsky, A. M., Appelbaum, P. S., Swartz, M. S., and Kessler, R. C. (2015) "Guns, Impulsive Angry Behavior, and Mental Disorders: Results from the National Comorbidity Survey Replication (Ncs-R)." *Behavioral Sciences & the Law* **33** (2-3), 199–212.

Swedler, D. I., Simmons, M. M., Dominici, F., and Hemenway, D. (2015) "Firearm Prevalence and Homicides of Law Enforcement Officers in the United States." *American Journal of Public Health* **105** (10), 2042–2048.

Tavernise, S. (2016) "Young Adolescents as Likely to Die from Suicide as from Traffic Accidents." *New York Times,* 3 November. [Online] Available at: https://www.nytimes.com/2016/11/04/health/suicide-adolescents-traffic-deaths.html?mcubz=1. [Accessed: 12 August 2017].

Tavernise, S. and Gebeloff, R. (2013) "Share of Homes with Guns Shows 4-Decade Decline." *New York Times*, 9 March. [Online] Available at: http://www. nytimes.com/2013/03/10/us/rate-of-gun-ownership-is-down-survey-shows. html?pagewanted=all. [Accessed: 31 May 2013].

Tavris, C. and Aronson, E. (2007) *Mistakes Were Made (but Not by Me): Why We Justify Foolish Beliefs, Bad Decisions, and Hurtful Acts*. New York: Harcourt.

Tversky, A. and Kahneman, D. (1974) "Judgment under Uncertainty: Heuristics and Biases." *Science* **185**, 1124–1131.

—— (1973) "Availability: A Heuristic for Judging Frequency and Probability." *Cognitive Psychology* **5** (2), 207–232.

Uniacke, S. (1996) *Permissible Killing: The Self-Defence Justification of Homicide*. Cambridge: Cambridge University Press.

United Nations (2008) "The Core International Human Rights Instruments." Geneva: Office of the High Commissioner for Human Rights. [Online] Available at: http://www.ohchr.org/EN/ProfessionalInterest/Pages/CoreInstruments. aspx. [Accessed: 20 July 2013].

United Nations General Assembly (1948) "Universal Declaration of Human Rights." New York: United Nations. [Online] Available at: http://www.un.org/ en/documents/udhr/index.shtml. [Accessed: 20 July 2013].

Valentine, M. (2017) "The NRA Would Like to Insure You Now." *Politico*. [Online] Available at: http://politi.co/2r6BGj4. [Accessed: 31 August 2017].

Wellford, C. F., Pepper, J. V., and Petrie, C. V. (eds.) (2004) *Firearms and Violence: A Critical Review*. New York: National Academy Press. [Online] Available at: http://www.nap.edu/catalog/10881.html. [Accessed: 8 September 2013].

Wenar, L. (2011) "Rights." *Stanford Encyclopedia of Philosophy*. Zalta, E. N. Stanford, CA: Stanford University. [Online] Available at: http://plato.stanford.edu/ archives/fall2011/entries/rights/. [Accessed: 26 July 2013].

Wheeler, S. C., III (2001) "Gun Violence and Fundamental Rights." *Criminal Justice Ethics* **20** (1), 1925.

—— (1999) "Arms as Insurance." *Public Affairs Quarterly* **13** (2), 111–129.

—— (1997) "Self-Defense: Rights and Coerced Risk-Acceptance." *Public Affairs Quarterly* **11** (4), 431–443.

Wilson, T. D. (2004) *Strangers to Ourselves: Discovering the Adaptive Unconscious*. Cambridge, MA: Harvard University Press.

INDEX